PENGUIN BOOKS
LEELA

As the daughter of the Indian scientist Dr Ramaiah Naidu and a French journalist mother, Leela Naidu grew up in a world full of interesting people and events. Hrishikesh Mukherjee's *Anuradha* (screened at the Berlin Film Festival) launched her film career that included Merchant–Ivory's *The Householder*, Pradip Krishen's *Electric Moon* and Shyam Benegal's *Trikaal*. Leela also made her own shorts and documentaries, including *A Certain Childhood*. In the early 1980s, she was Ramnath Goenka's communications manager, and later editor of *Society* and managing editor of *Keynote*.

Leela's story was completed shortly before her untimely death in August 2009.

Jerry Pinto is a poet and journalist based in Mumbai. His published works include *Surviving Women* (2000); *Helen: The Life and Times of a Bollywood H-Bomb* (2006), for which he won the National Award for the Best Book on Cinema; a collection of poetry, *Asylum* (2004); and a novel for young people, *A Bear for Felicia* (2008). He is the editor of *Reflected in Water: Writings on Goa* (2006). He has also co-edited *Bombay, Meri Jaan: Writings on Mumbai* (2003) with Naresh Fernandes and *Confronting Love: Poems* (2005) with Arundhathi Subramaniam. He is on the board of MelJol, an NGO that works in the child rights space.

Leela
A PATCHWORK LIFE

LEELA NAIDU WITH JERRY PINTO

PENGUIN BOOKS

PENGUIN BOOKS

Published by the Penguin Group

Penguin Books India Pvt. Ltd, 11 Community Centre, Panchsheel Park, New Delhi 110 017, India

Penguin Group (USA) Inc., 375 Hudson Street, New York, New York 10014, USA

Penguin Group (Canada), 90 Eglinton Avenue East, Suite 700, Toronto, Ontario, M4P 2Y3, Canada (a division of Pearson Penguin Canada Inc.)

Penguin Books Ltd, 80 Strand, London WC2R 0RL, England

Penguin Ireland, 25 St Stephen's Green, Dublin 2, Ireland (a division of Penguin Books Ltd)

Penguin Group (Australia), 250 Camberwell Road, Camberwell, Victoria 3124, Australia (a division of Pearson Australia Group Pty Ltd)

Penguin Group (NZ), 67 Apollo Drive, Rosedale, Auckland 0632, New Zealand (a division of Pearson New Zealand Ltd)

Penguin Group (South Africa) (Pty) Ltd, 24 Sturdee Avenue, Rosebank, Johannesburg 2196, South Africa

Penguin Books Ltd, Registered Offices: 80 Strand, London WC2R 0RL, England

First published in Viking by Penguin Books India 2010
Published in Penguin Books 2012

Copyright © Jerry Pinto 2010

All photographs provided by Leela Naidu from her personal collection

All rights reserved

10 9 8 7 6 5 4 3 2 1

The views and opinions expressed in this book are the authors' own and the facts are as reported by them which have been verified to the extent possible, and the publishers are not in any way liable for the same.

ISBN 9780143418641

Typeset in Adobe Garamond by InoSoft Systems, Noida
Printed at Sanat Printers, Kundli

This book is sold subject to the condition that it shall not, by way of trade or otherwise, be lent, resold, hired out, or otherwise circulated without the publisher's prior written consent in any form of binding or cover other than that in which it is published and without a similar condition including this condition being imposed on the subsequent purchaser and without limiting the rights under copyright reserved above, no part of this publication may be reproduced, stored in or introduced into a retrieval system, or transmitted in any form or by any means (electronic, mechanical, photocopying, recording or otherwise), without the prior written permission of both the copyright owner and the above-mentioned publisher of this book.

Contents

FOREWORD **VII**

PROLOGUE **1**

One: THE NAKED COUNT ON THE LAWN **7**

Two: FROM FIVE GARDENS TO PARIS **12**

Three: OF RACISTS AND OTHER ANIMALS **19**

Four: ANOTHER HOME **36**

Five: PARIS BY RENOIR **41**

Six: THREE RUBBER BRAS AND A YELLOW NOSE **53**

Seven: 'WHO AM I PLAYING, LEELA?' **63**

Eight: A MAN POSSESSED **74**

Nine: 'SHE HAS NO BAD ANGLES' **80**

Ten: LEELA NAIDU, PRODUCER **87**

Eleven: AMONG THE NAXALITES **105**

Twelve: CAUTION: LEILA KHALED IS COMING **115**

Thirteen: BREATHLESS VICTORY   **122**

Fourteen: TRAVELLING WITH DOM MORAES   **126**

Fifteen: TRANSLATING IONESCO   **141**

Sixteen: LEELA NAIDU, EDITOR   **150**

Seventeen: 'HAVE YOU STOPPED ACTING?'   **158**

Eighteen: THE BRITISH ON A HUNGER STRIKE IN THE LAND OF THE MAHATMA   **163**

Nineteen: SEASON OF MISTS AND MELLOW FRUITFULNESS   **170**

LEELA'S EPILOGUE   **179**

Foreword
Writing Leela

The last time I saw Leela Naidu, she was sitting up in bed. She had on a faded nightgown and the bedclothes, relics of a visit from one of her grandsons, sported cheerful cartoon animals. But she extended her hand with the grace of a dowager duchess in exile and smiled upon me. The room brightened and the world turned into a gracious and charming place for a moment.

The first time I saw Leela Naidu? I don't think any forty something man can remember when he first saw Leela. She was there, an iconic image, a presence, a reminder of what feminine beauty could be about, if it were not saturated and enhanced and made to look like a parody of itself. But it wasn't just that. Beauty, as she points out somewhere in the book we wrote together, is simply one of those gifts of deoxyribonucleic acid. It's an accident, a happy accident, but nothing more than that. The lives of hundreds of supermodels and starlets show that you can be beautiful and it won't get you much more than five minutes of fame. Leela was different because she had a very sharp mind behind that porcelain face with its flawless skin and greying head of hair. She was different because she knew that when she entered a room, she owned it—how could she not know? She had been beautiful since the time she was eight years old or thereabouts—but she never let you think you were a devotee, even if you were looking at her with your heart in your eyes. She turned her attention on you and she made you feel that her beauty was a special gift to you, that she was only the steward of its ability to make you think of chocolate and jazz, of the inside of a shell and the morning monsoon sky.

The first time I met Leela Naidu was on 1 May 1990. I had gone to interview Dom Moraes about a book of poetry, *Serendip*; it had been published in a limited signed edition, a publishing first in India. But more importantly, it was his first work in verse after an interval of nearly seventeen years. I was writing for the *Free Press Journal*, then edited by Janardhan Thakur. He was a friend of the family and when I arrived, he was sitting with the Moraeses. I had heard much about these two: Dom and Leela, Leela and Dom.

'*Un coup de foudre*,' was how an old-timer described their first meeting. 'She came to a party with Zafar Hai. Dom was alone. Dom and Leela looked at each other and left together. That was it.'

'Nonsense,' said Leela, when I told her about this. But so many people have told me this story that I have put it in as one of those Leela legends. She has told her own version of the Dom and Leela legend in these pages, with a curious mixture of affection and contempt so I won't belabour the point. Anyway, at that time, it was said to be a marriage made in heaven. But I could smell unhappiness in the air.

How could they be unhappy? She was one of the most beautiful women in the world, according to *Vogue*. He was one of the most talented of poets and writers. They had known each other since they were infants. He was writing poetry again. She had acted in *Electric Moon*, said to be something of a critical success. They were living in Sargent House, a beautiful colonial building on a quiet street of Colaba Causeway, all high ceilings and teak furniture, paintings by S.H. Raza and Jatin Das on the walls. Selvam, faithful retainer, and the only domestic help in Mumbai to be described as a major domo, turned out perfect coffee for all of us. It was served in elegant crockery and the sum total paralysed me. I was sure I would commit some awful social faux pas by virtue of just being there.

Leela must have sensed this because she was inordinately kind. She said that she enjoyed my writing.

'Where have you read his writing?' Dom asked.

Leela dismissed this with an airy hand. We talked about food. Dom told a story about how he and Leela had taken Stephen Spender to a restaurant in a five-star hotel and the British poet had ordered a steak. It had arrived so tough, that his fork slid off it and it flew off his plate and landed on the floor.

Thakur suggested that she write a column for the *FPJ* about food. She should 'bust open' the myths of the five-star hotels, he said. She grinned and suggested that she and I could do a joint column. But it would have to be anonymous.

'Would you pay the bills?' she asked Thakur.

'No, no,' he said and I like to think it was not because he did not see the sense in anonymous reviewing but because the management would never agree.

Leela wrote in my diary, 'Pot it! Against all those stingy-mingy editors who have lost "our" (yours and mine) coup! We shall meet, we shall eat—at least at my place which you can "bust".'

Then she gave me an orchid in an egg-cup. For some reason this seemed like the perfect gesture.

~

I met her infrequently after that, mainly because Dom was around and Dom wanted to be the poetic father figure. I do not take well to patronage. It makes me want to bite someone. I was pleased when he said he would like to help me publish my poems but I didn't want to be a drinking buddy. When Leela and I met, which was infrequent because I was still working my way past my own inadequacies, we drank coffee, smoked cigarettes and talked about nothing of any consequence.

I heard that Dom had left Leela in a roundabout 'You do know . . .' way. I went over and she wept on my shoulder for a while and then wiped her tears, sniffling into a man's hankie.

'My father's,' she said with a watery smile. 'He's not good enough to blow my nose into.'

I tried to visit her more regularly after that. One day, she was giggling merrily.

'I've been reading *Henrietta*,' she said, referring to the autobiography of Henrietta Moraes, the woman once described as the only female queen of Soho, muse to Francis Bacon, wife to Dom Moraes. 'Do you know she says that Dom said he was going out for cigarettes and never came back? Why didn't someone tell me that before I married him?'

'Would you have listened?' I asked.

She cocked her head, a gesture that made her look like an intelligent sparrow considering the world view of a crow.

'You are such a brute,' she said appreciatively and my ego bloomed and shrivelled simultaneously.

She was that kind of lady.

~

We began writing the book some years ago, I can't even remember when. I thought I would have the date in a diary somewhere but I don't. I have an entry late in 2003 that says 'Leela finally' which could possibly mean that we had finally begun the work of writing.

On the first day, I remember she had a recording machine on the table. 'There's a journalist who wants me to record myself. He says he will turn it into a book,' she said. 'He gave me this machine and he said I should just speak into it. Then he went away.'

We both looked at the machine.

'Do you think you should do this book with him?' I asked eventually.

'No, no,' she said. 'I'm just telling you about it. I'm going to send the machine back to him. With a nice note. That would be *convenable, non?*'

Leela was bilingual. She spoke excellent French and she spoke excellent English but she often spoke them both at the same time. This was not always at the level of words. Sometimes, it would be an intonation, an inflection that would remind me that somewhere she was thinking in French as well.

We met every week, once a week for nearly three years. Then, in the fourth year, I started writing drafts. We went through seven or eight drafts until we were done. We worked through the calamities of an old house—a fire escape that collapsed in the night, the death of a lime tree in the garden that Leela tended with such love, a slab falling from the ceiling in the kitchen. We worked through health problems—a fall, a cough, an attack of influenza. We worked through personal problems—the worst being the death of her daughter, Priya.

'Do you want to talk about all this?' I asked her, once. She had been crying quietly and we were both a bit soggy.

'All this?' She thought about it for a bit. 'There's been quite a bit of all this in my life. And I have never wanted to parade my grief in public.'

'But you have talked about it,' I pointed out. 'It's in magazines, newspapers.'

'They took advantage of a relationship,' she said.

'You must have known they would print.'

'I did not.'

'You must have wanted to tell.'

'I don't now,' she said, firmly. 'There's no point.'

We talked a little about pain, about narratives of pain and about narratives of feminine pain.

And then we were done.

At the end of this book, she insisted on appending an epilogue. She bid her adieux. And a week later, she was gone.

An odd week followed. Many journalists seemed to want to memorialise her but few seemed to have any idea what they wanted to say. I received this rather strange email from a journalist who said she was working for a reputable broadsheet:

Mr Pinto,

As I mentioned in the few texts we exchanged earlier, the *Indian Express* intends to do a Sunday feature on late Ms Leela Naidu. Not much of her life is documented and since she kept a low profile, limiting her social life to a few close friends, I am challenged in terms of sources.

However, I read in the *Times of India* about your book on Ms Naidu and hence seek your help. While a phone conversation would have allowed more space for an exchange of ideas and views, you say that looks tough. Hence, I'd like to initiate this with the following questions. I have one more request: we are also looking for some photographs from the various stages of her life and Mr Ranjit Hoskoté, whom I happened to speak to earlier, mentioned you might be able to guide me on that front too.

Would you be able to tell me about her early years—birth, upbringing (especially since her mother was French and father Indian), education and how she ventured into modelling? Where did Dom Moraes feature in her early years?

What were her interests and personal life like, off-screen? How did she keep herself occupied, what were her literary interests, et al.

She married early but what made her end her career in the film industry?

What ailed her marriages?

How did she survive financially after Moraes moved on?

What was the last decade of her life like?

Who were her close friends and did she have any friends in the film industry?

I know I ask a wide range of questions and that to answer them all and in entirety may not be possible for you, hence, I would appreciate whatever you can share with me. Will appreciate [*sic*] any guidance in terms of direction and whom I could speak to.

Thank you for your time.

Sincerely,

I shall omit the name to be kind. But there were some journalists who did an exceptional job of putting her in perspective. Vikram Doctor wrote in the *Economic Times*, 'Naidu was one of a group of beautiful Indian women who, from the Forties to the early Sixties, helped create an idea of a beautiful, elegant and accomplished new nation. This included Rani Gayatri Devi of Jaipur, the other name that people remember from that "10 most beautiful women" list and Nayantara Sahgal, the writer and Jawaharlal Nehru's niece.

'All these women shared a certain style. While unmistakably Indian and nearly always dressed in saris, there was also a Western air to them as well. They all had Western connections (Naidu's mother was French) or had lived abroad (Gayatri Devi came from the relatively liberal Cooch Behar royal family, which had let her travel abroad at an early age, while Sahgal had been allowed to study in the US), and they presented themselves in a mix of Indian and European styles—saris and Indian jewellery, but worn with Western sophistication.'

Art critic, curator and poet Ranjit Hoskoté, wrote in the *Hindustan Times*, 'Those who knew her well often voiced the feeling that Naidu had never been able to fulfil the potential for which her birth, upbringing and education had equipped her.

'Indeed, she belonged to that rapidly disappearing class of people, of whom words like birth and upbringing can be used without irony. They recognised the role they were meant to play in a civilisation rather than a society, even if circumstances conspired to prevent them from playing that role in full measure. It is possible that Naidu was doomed by her membership of a lost intermediate generation of Indian women, who came of age after the structures of feudal and colonial patriarchy had collapsed, but before the advent of feminism made it possible for women to shape and manage careers in the public sphere as agents of their own choice and destiny. Leela Naidu was among the last of Mumbai's truly Romantic figures. As with all such figures, the legend came to overwhelm the life.'

And because Leela would not have wanted anyone to go away without a chuckle, I'm not going to let this end on a sombre note.

Everyone, it seemed, had a Leela Naidu story. I had only to mention that I was helping her write her autobiography and someone would say: 'But you must hear Salman tell his Leela Naidu story.' Or it would be, 'You must hear Suketu tell his Leela Naidu story.'

And here is the Salman Rushdie story, told to me on a cool night in Jaipur: 'Dom Moraes had done a rude piece about my work, which had appeared in the *Sunday Observer*. But when I came to Bombay, he called and said that he had been misquoted and could we meet for a drink? I agreed but thought I would check with Vinod Mehta. "How can we have misquoted him?" Vinod asked, outraged. "He wrote the piece. I have his hard copy here with me." But I decided that I would let it go. If he wanted to extend the peace pipe, I could take a puff too. We met at the President, around noon, and we talked about this and that, while he put away several large whiskies. Then he suggested that I should go home with him for lunch. I didn't really want to but I thought, "Leela Naidu!" so I agreed. We left together, after he'd had another whisky, and we went back to their flat at Sargent House. We arrived, Dom drank, Dom expatiated on this and that including his war writing on Vietnam, we waited, nobody appeared, we waited some more, Dom drank some more. He then disappeared into the depths of the apartment, then he disappeared into another room and suddenly there was an explosion of feminine rage. The walls shook as Leela raged at him in at least three languages. Then there was a silence. I waited some more. Then the bearer came and asked if I would like to have lunch. I said I would leave but he insisted. I asked where Dom was and he said, quite calmly, "Saahab behosh ho gaya". I ate a chicken cutlet and chips in solitary splendour wondering if Leela Naidu would show. She did not. I was then offered dessert, declined it, and fled. And I never met Leela.'

This is Suketu Mehta, on Leela Naidu. 'When I first moved back to Bombay I was staying in a sort of Gujju ghetto on Napean Sea Road, an old building with a lot of garbage strewn around.

I thought I would have a dinner for some of the people I was meeting. Leela Naidu came and sat down on a sofa early in the evening. At some point she stamped her exquisite chappal-clad foot hard on the floor. She did not get up from the sofa. Someone brought her her wine there and someone took dinner over to her. She sat unmoving through the evening and into the night. One by one, the guests drifted away until it was only Leela, sitting on the sofa. Finally, she asked whether it was now only the family. I said it was. She lifted her foot. Beneath it was a cockroach, which she had squashed to save me embarrassment in front of my dinner guests. We both regarded the flattened bug. Then Leela said, "I think it's fainted."

~

There's a Leela-shaped hole in my life.

JERRY PINTO
Mumbai
An arid day in August 2009

Prologue

I am fortunate to have begun writing this account of my life at a time when no one believes that there is a single truth or a single version of a life. Had I been writing some decades ago, I might have been forced to offer an extended apologia for my decisions. But my friends tell me that literary critics have now come to the conclusion that no one can give a full account of their lives any more than anyone can document every moment in the life of a universe. It seems to me that a great many trees would have been saved had they come to this conclusion earlier and the doorstop-sized biographies and autobiographies to which we have been subjected might simply have been pared down to what matters. And had they paid attention to ancient wisdom, they would have known that no human being may be summed up in words. The Talmud puts it beautifully when it says, 'You do not kill a man, you kill a universe.' Nor does one sum up a person, not even the person one is.

So this book is about what matters to a certain Leela Naidu. I qualify that because I believe that the person narrating this is the Leela I am at this point. I may have been another person earlier and I may change yet again. The person I was earlier may have had another view of the life she led; the Leela to come may see things differently. I give her leave to do so.

With that mad visionary William Blake, I believe, *Joy and woe are woven fine/ A clothing for the soul divine./ Under every grief and pine/ Runs a joy with silken twine.*

I believe this to be true of every life and mine has been no exception. To tell one's life fairly then would be to tell the sorrows and the joys in equal measure.

I have had my fair share of pain. I was married twice, once to Tilak Raj Oberoi of the Oberoi family that has done much for the hospitality industry in India; and the second time to the poet Dom Moraes. The marriages did not work. I do not flinch from the memories I have nor do I consciously relive them. (What dreams bring is another matter.) I do not see what use it would be to recount my 'trials and tribulations', except to add yet another narrative of feminine pain to the ones that are already extant. I offer no disrespect to those women. I respect the choices they make in the narratives they shape out of the raw material of their lives. I expect the same respect for the choices I make.

I would willingly bare the scabs on my soul were I to suspect that there would be some value in so doing. When I was beginning my career in cinema, the socialist writer and columnist Khwaja Ahmed Abbas, who wrote some of Raj Kapoor's early films, said to me, 'You are too young to be an actress. You have not suffered enough.' I suppose I could have asked him how much I was supposed to suffer before I could qualify. I suppose I could have offered to sleep on a bed of nails for a month or to wear a hair shirt. I suppose I could have asked whether he had suffered enough to be a writer. I like to think these witty retorts were only held back by my respect for his seniority but I suspect that I was simply left dumbstruck by the notion that there is a certain value to suffering.

There are some religious traditions, I know, that place a high value on suffering. I myself was born into a family that did not make too much out of organised religion. My father was a Hindu by birth, my mother had been born a Catholic.

They left me to choose, stipulating only that I should make my decision when I was seven. When I did, I opted for Sufism.

I remember the conversation I had with the Abbé Pierre, the religious preceptor at the private Catholic school in Geneva to which I was sent.

'In India,' he told the class once, 'they revere crocodiles and venerate fish. Their gods are wood and stone.'

If ever there was a misreading of the inclusive tradition of Hinduism, if ever there was a more narrow-minded reading of the representation of the Ganga as a crocodile and the Matsya avatar of Vishnu, I have yet to hear it.

I was young but I was ready to stand my ground against such notions. 'But, Monsieur l'Abbé,' I said. 'The statue of the Virgin Mary in the chapel is also made of wood.'

He spluttered his contempt of this remark. Of course, his statue was only a representation and a mnemonic, a reminder of his beloved Mother Mary. It was not an idol, it was a way of focussing attention on the Divine. I believe that even as he said it, he knew he was digging a hole for himself, so he changed the subject.

'Have you been baptised?' he asked.

I told him that I had not.

'Then why is it that the only child I see in the chapel every day is you?' he asked.

I could not put it into words but I think he knew that I responded to the shelter and the silence of the chapel. I responded to the beauty of the faith that had built it, not to the crudeness of that very faith's attacks on those different from it. We eventually grew to be great friends and when I told him that I had decided to be a Sufi, he asked why.

This time I had thought it out. I remembered the candles that the Sufis lit in their room in Geneva. I remembered the candles that represented the major faiths of the world—Christianity, Judaism, Islam, Buddhism, Hinduism, tribal faiths—and one for the unknown religions. Ali Khan, the cousin of Sufi teacher and celebrated musician Inayat Khan, initiated me into Sufism. When he visited Geneva I would accompany him on the piano. I thought of the warmth he generated, the extraordinary generosity of spirit. But while I recognised these things with a child's instincts, I had not the vocabulary to express them. As the Bible says, when one is a child, one speaks as a child.

'Everyone else wants me to choose one apple when I love all apples,' I said. And as I said it, I knew I needed another metaphor.

'One apple is generally enough for a little girl like you,' he said.

'Everyone else wants me to choose one colour when I love all colours,' I said.

He harrumphed again, but we remained friends and I still visited the chapel.

A friend of mine has suggested that it is also because of my wandering life. I was born in Bombay, and by the time I was seven, I had lived in two other cities: Paris and Geneva. The Sufis, he suggested, were also wanderers. But I think what attracted me to Sufism was its passionate commitment to love, not the *agape* of the New Testament, but love in the here-and-now, God as the beloved who must be sought, who can be found, and who often leaves one for a while to experience the sweet sorrow of parting. And there was the music and the celebration of God that it so beautifully expressed. Pain is the antithesis of celebration.

I remember asking my father why we should feel pain.

'If a child puts her hand in the fire, she feels pain and she learns that she should not do it again,' he said. Well, yes, but how does one know what will hurt and what will not? The only way is to find out for oneself.

With the benefit of hindsight, I have discovered that, as a species, we do not learn from the mistakes of others, especially in matters of the heart. Perhaps it is the belief that we all have when we are young, the belief in a personal exemption from the workings of nature or karma or what you will. Perhaps it is that we cannot believe that we will be so foolish, so foolhardy, so ill advised as the person we are reading about. Whatever the reason, humankind does not learn from history and I believe that the readers of angina monologues learn nothing.

This then is my story in the way I should wish to tell it. There are other versions because there are other people in whose minds I have a presence. This is the Leela I know. She had an eventful life by her own understanding of it and she thinks you might like to hear about it.

~

Tolstoy's *Anna Karenina* begins with the immortal and oft-quoted lines, 'All happy families are happy in the same way, all unhappy families are unhappy in their own way.' With due respect to Tolstoy, I am not sure whether that is how it works. It suggests that happiness is a bland monotonous state and unhappiness is the only state worth investigating. Or writing about.

Of course, Indians are only now discovering that they had unhappy childhoods. It was perfectly common for adults when I was growing up to talk about how their parents were tyrannical, cold aloof presences ('they taught me values') and how their schools were chambers of horrors ('it toughened me up') and then to add with a reminiscent and sentimental sigh, 'Ah, the golden days of childhood.'

People did speak like that. And they did not see the contradictions. I would often wonder at it. Every child is a bundle of feelings, the most important ones of which are helplessness and self-interest. If your father beat you for every minor misdemeanour and your school made you take cold baths at some unearthly hour and then forced you to do physical exercise that verged on hard labour, both these feelings must be outraged. No child wants to have values beaten into him or her; no child wants to run around a playground fifty times even if it builds them into wiry Spartans. But to say any of this would mean to cast some doubt on one's parents and no one doubted their parents when I was growing up.

Nor did I doubt mine.

Suffice it to say that I was happy and that I am perfectly willing to accept that this is only nostalgia. But as for presenting my parents in the best light possible, I don't think I need to do that. They were good parents and good people to begin with. But if they had had flaws, I would have still loved them for that is the nature of the child. And as an adult one should know that to look for perfection in others is somewhat silly when one is constantly reminded of one's own imperfections. As an adult looking back, I can only remember being treated with respect. Neither of them ever beat me or inflicted any cruel or unusual punishment on my person. When they felt the need to correct me, they appealed to my sense of reason and my sense of right and wrong.

So I will begin randomly with a naked Russian in a French garden.

2 July 2009

ONE

The Naked Count on the Lawn

I do not remember much about her, but my mother told me that her mother had eyes that were the blue of forget-me-nots. I like to think of her sitting in her salon, looking out over her garden, perhaps sipping a cup of camomile tea when she heard the door-pull on the front door.

A minute or so later she heard a thud.

She went to the door and found that the maid who had answered the doorbell had fainted clean away.

Outside, a tall man was standing. He seemed abstracted, as if he were thinking of something else. He was also completely naked.

The French have a word for my grandmother's response. With perfect *sang-froid*, she invited her visitor in and provided him with my grandfather's dressing gown. Then she offered him some tea and petit fours and they began to converse as though it were an everyday occurrence that a tall white man should turn up nude on one's doorstep.

After a seemly interval, she asked her visitor's name.

'I am the Count Yousoupoff,' he said and there was a moment's silence as my grandmother digested this information. 'I did not shoot him,' he added softly.

The Prince Felix Yousoupoff (or Yusupov) will best be remembered by history as one of the men who killed Grigori Yefimovich

Rasputin, the 'mad monk' who held Russia to ransom since he had convinced Tsar Nicholas and Tsarina Alexandra that he could cure their son and heir of the haemophilia that he had inherited through Queen Victoria.

Having decided that Rasputin's influence over the Tsarina made him too dangerous to the Empire, a group of nobles apparently lured Rasputin to the Moika Palace, which belonged to the maternal family of Prince Yusupov, who had taken on his mother's name to prevent it from dying out. The more fanciful accounts of Rasputin's death state that he was served cakes and vodka laced with enough cyanide to kill ten men. Now, as far as I know, cyanide is supposed to be a swift acting poison but according to the legend, Rasputin was not affected. He is even said to have started munching and swallowing the crystal glasses in which the vodka had been served. Yusupov is then said to have gone upstairs, fetched his revolver and shot the Siberian cleric through the chest. Rasputin fell. A half an hour or so later when Yusupov returned to check the body (or as some versions go, Yusupov came back for his jacket), Rasputin sprang to his feet and began to throttle Yusupov, who fled in horror and told the other conspirators.

Heavily drugged by this time, Rasputin attempted his escape. He bolted outside and ran across the courtyard toward the gate, threatening that he would tell everything to the Tsarina. Another conspirator shot three bullets that passed Rasputin, then he shot two more which hit the monk. The conspirators then clubbed him unconscious and flung him into the icy Neva River, but there was no splash. Rasputin had fallen on the ice (it was winter at this time), so they went down and cut a hole in the ice and stuffed him through it into the icy water. They were finally satisfied that the 'Enemy of the State' was dead.

Three days later the body of Rasputin—poisoned, shot three times and badly beaten—was recovered from the river and autopsied. The cause of death was drowning. His arms were apparently found in an upright position, as if he had tried to claw his way out from under the ice.

Of course, historians have challenged almost everything about this story. And here was Yusupov sitting in my grandparents' villa in the shadow of the Jura Alps and saying that he had not done what legend said he had done.

Then there was another knock on the door and a clamour. I can imagine my grandmother girding her loins for a further incursion of strange men. But it was only the distraught keepers from the château opposite. They reclaimed the Prince, who had slipped away from them.

'I will return,' he said, bowing in an elegant Gallic fashion. The Russian court was as French as it could make itself.

'Please do,' said my grandmother, relieved that it was simply a madman with delusions of grandeur.

Later, she found that this was no pretender to royalty and fame. It was indeed the Prince Yusupov who had visited her. That day was a Thursday, the day when Rasputin had been killed. Every Thursday, when he was haunted by Rasputin's eyes that had turned fluorescent green from the arsenic he had ingested, he would visit her for a while and they would drink tea together and he would sit silently, trying perhaps to sort out the past.

That is the earliest story told to me that I remember. The other one that concerns my grandfather came to me in a roundabout fashion when I was a young girl of about eight, living in Geneva. Those were more innocent days and parents did not hesitate to send their children out, unattended. One day, at the park, I saw an old man staring at me intently, but with a trace of confusion in his eyes.

'Good afternoon,' I said hesitantly.

'Marthe?' he said.

'That is my mother's name, sir,' I said.

The confusion cleared. 'So it is her daughter,' he said, 'Marthe's daughter.'

'Do you know my mother?' I asked, excited.

'I knew her, little one, but only as the daughter of my employer. It has been many years now . . .'

But I was having none of it. I dragged him off home and although Maman responded with her customary good manners, I could see an unspoken 'Oh mon Dieu' hovering on her lips as I dragged an elderly stranger into her living room.

My grandfather Mange had, in his time, been the sole importer and purveyor of American threshing machines in Europe. It was at his factory that the old man had worked.

He chatted about my grandfather of whom he had many fond memories. He told me how my grandfather had been a great shot of wild game and how the French army had wanted him to join up in the First World War, even though he was well into his forties and fast nearing the outer limit of the age for conscription. However, my grandfather was committed to the notion of non-violence and he had instead offered his Rolls Royce and driver to fetch and carry supplies to the front, the old man said.

Indeed, I had heard of stories of my grandfather's valour. He had never fired a shot throughout the war, but he had risked his life to rescue the fallen and the wounded from the no-man's-land between the German and French lines in the Vosges. He had been buried alive thrice and after he had been dug out the third time and was recovering in hospital, some generals who wanted to give him a medal of honour visited him.

My grandfather refused the medal. 'I am proud that I have never fired on a German,' he told the generals, 'I am proud that I have never killed someone's father or someone's son or someone's brother.'

They knew of his bravery and his service to the army. They could not make sense of him. But here was a living link with my grandfather.

'And did you know about the young man who walked into the factory once and your grandpapa offered him a job?'

I may have been young but I could smell a good story coming.

'No, I don't,' I said and settled down to listen.

'Well, many years before the war, a young man walked in and asked for work. He was hired although he was Italian and although he seemed a little cocky. He worked for a while and then one day, your grandfather heard a terrible scream, a scream of mortal agony . . .'

I shivered.

'The young man had had a disagreement with another worker. He had been working near the furnace of the foundry and he had seized a red-hot metal rod and banged it down on the hand of the other worker. Your grandfather first despatched the injured worker to the hospital. Then he called the Italian to his office. "You are not fit to work in teams," he told the man as he gave him his marching orders.'

I wondered whether that was the end of the story.

'Do you know what the name of the Italian was?'

I didn't know. How could I?

'Benito Mussolini,' he said triumphantly.

TWO

From Five Gardens to Paris

I once showed a friend a picture of my mother. He said, 'She looks determined.' She was and I inherited that from her. And so, when at the age of three, I decided that I wanted to go to school, I found my way to school.

We were living at Five Gardens then, a quiet, leafy part of central Bombay. It has not changed much, I am told. In one of the gardens—a maidan really—the good Jesuits had set up an open-air school. I have no idea why they were there, but there were tents and there were students and there were teachers and very soon, there was Leela.

I wandered around until I found what looked like my age group. The priest in charge was slightly bemused.

'Where have you come from?'

I pointed to my home. When he tried to take me home, I refused to go.

'I want to go to school,' I told him.

Perhaps I made a refreshing change from the whining schoolboys with 'shining morning faces, creeping like snails, unwillingly to school' but he sat me down in a corner with the youngest students and told me to colour a butterfly and then pin it up somewhere.

'Hsst,' said the little boy next to me as I finished my butterfly. We were then supposed to stick them on to a board with drawing pins.

I looked up.

He pointed at his lap. He had opened his shop and what looked to me like a grub was on display. I had no idea what I was looking at but it didn't look very attractive. Ever interested in raising the general aesthetic standards of the environment, I tried to improve things and stuck my butterfly on it.

With a drawing pin, of course.

When my mother came to collect me, I was sitting with my nose in the corner. It seemed to be evident that I was already in trouble.

'What has she been doing?' she asked.

The priest found it difficult to answer.

A year later, I finally went to my first school, Cathedral School in Colaba at the southern tip of the island city of Mumbai. I had a picture of Chopin tucked into the pocket of my pinafore. Chopin was my first love. I loved his music and I wanted to learn to play the piano.

In that I was like my mother. She too had wanted to learn music but her father was having none of it. But my grandmother was more sympathetic and found her a teacher to give her lessons. Since there was no piano in their home, Grand-maman and the driver got together and created a little keyboard out of cardboard so that Maman could practise. She was so good at it that she was chosen to perform at a local festival at Divonne-les-Bains. My grandmother took her husband to it and he was surprised to see his daughter play beautifully. And so she got her piano.

My problem was diffidence. My mother would play the piano and I would watch her and yearn to play and wonder how to tell her that I wanted to play. By this time, we were in Sargent House in Colaba. Beneath us lived Harry Littler, one of the last relicts of the Raj, one of those who stayed on. He was a piano teacher but it was well known that he had no time for four-year-olds.

One day, I was tinkling away when my mother was out and the doorbell rang.

'Who is playing the piano?' he demanded gruffly and walked into the room. 'I know it isn't Marthe; I know her playing . . .'

I sat frozen on the stool.

'You,' he said.

Then he turned and left. But the next day, Maman asked me if I wanted to learn the piano for the so very stern Harry Littler was ready to take me on as a pupil.

I wanted desperately to learn to play something for my mother's birthday. I wanted it to be beautiful for her. So I learnt a simplified piece by Chopin and I played it to her on her birthday when her friends were over. When I finished, they were all trying not to laugh.

'Thank you, chérie,' she said, with a slight smile. 'But why would you play a funeral march on my birthday?'

Perhaps I knew even then that there was a strain of sadness, of melancholia, somewhere inside her.

We moved to Paris soon afterwards where I continued to learn ballet with Madame Primakova, a Russian émigrée. My parents encouraged me in my enthusiasms. Neither ever insisted that I should do what they had done. My father, Dr Ramaiah Naidu, was a scientist, a physicist and a radiologist. His world was the world of thought, of nuclear physics. He had worked his way up, running away from home to go to Aurobindo Ghosh's fledgling ashram in Pondicherry. From there, he went on to Shantiniketan where he taught mathematics for a while until he went to Benares Hindu University for his master's degree in the sciences. He was offered a scholarship to England, but he turned it down because he wanted no favours from the colonial rulers of India. Instead, he wrote to Madame Curie and was accepted into the Sorbonne where he completed his doctorate.

'The day of the results,' he told me, 'we all went to the university. I got through the press of bodies to the notice board. I looked for my name at the bottom where in India, what we call the "pass classes" would be listed. I wasn't among them. I looked among those who had passed in the second class. I was still not among them. I looked among those who had secured a first class. No Naidu. My heart was sinking. I had not expected to fail but it seemed . . . then I got to the top of the list and I found, to my great surprise, that my name led all the rest.'

Later, he is said to have helped establish the foundations of medical physics. He was a post-doctoral fellow of Madame Curie and when she died, he was running her laboratory. Later, he was the first medical physicist at the Tata Memorial Hospital, Bombay, where he installed a radon production facility. He had implemented a similar facility at the Sloan Kettering Memorial Institute in New York. He introduced me to the wonder of the natural world, explaining everything to me without ever being condescending, but I can never remember him even suggesting that I should study science.

My mother was a journalist with *Le Petit Democrat Populaire*. She mentioned that someone had once thrown a hand grenade into the office.

'Weren't you scared?' I asked.

'I did not have the time to be scared,' said my mother.

She met my father when she was sent to cover the Second Round Table Conference; he was the head of the Cambridge Students' Union. If all this sounds like the bare bones of their relationship, it is because I did not ask my parents questions. I felt that would be impertinent of me. What I knew of their lives before me, or before their marriage, has been pieced together from what they chose to tell me.

But as a child, my world was full of interesting people and events. For instance, Sarojini Naidu may have been the 'nightingale of India', the first woman to be president of the Indian National Congress and the first woman to become the governor of an Indian state. But to me she was a well-beloved aunt, so large that she could not fit easily in most of our chairs. She loved her food and Maman filled a huge tiffin box and sent it to her whenever she travelled. One day, when she was living at the Bhulabhai Desai House on the Bhulabhai Desai Road in south Mumbai, she called me to her. She handed me a box of chocolates and a bunch of gladioli from a vase.

'Now go out to the outhouse and see Mickey Mouse,' she said.

I had my marching orders and I went to the outhouse. I knocked on the door and was called in. I was still expecting to meet the Disney character; instead, sitting on the bed was Mahatma Gandhi.

'You are not Mickey Mouse!' I said.

'No?' Gandhiji asked.

'Your ears are big but they're not big enough.'

'Is that all?' he asked and turned around to put on the side light.

'And you don't have a tail.'

He laughed at that and put on the light.

'So I am not Mickey Mouse,' Gandhiji said, 'but who am I?'

'You are Gandhiji,' I said.

I put the flowers down and gave him the chocolates. He took them and began to eat them immediately, as happy as a schoolboy with a box of tuck.

'How do you know who I am?' he said.

I don't remember if I had explained or not, but I do remember shouting *Gandhiji ki jai* even in my two-wheeler pram. Later I had organized a ceremonial burning of solar topis made out of paper as part of my protest against the British Raj. But I do remember his strong arms around me as he hugged me. A few years later, in Geneva, I came home from school one day to find my mother looking pale.

'Leela,' she said, 'something terrible has happened.' That was the day Gandhiji was assassinated.

We wept together for the loss of the nation but I also wept for the thin man with the warm eyes and the hug that made you feel loved. The political without the personal often seems to me to be barren.

My parents' ability to allow for difference attracted a wide range of people. They extended this courtesy to me too. They were willing to allow me to choose my path. I cannot ever remember even a suggestion as to what I should do. Their only requirement was that I persevere.

'Will you see it through?' was the only question my father would ask when I announced that I wanted to learn something new. If I said I would it was assumed that I would keep my word. Whether it was the piano or ballet or horse-riding the same question was asked and when I had promised, the necessary arrangements were made. I kept my side of the bargain.

In Paris, Daddy had to go to the hospital where they were going to treat him for artificial blood cancer. He had been exposed to radium. What saved him, he said, was his habit of walking. To oxygenate his blood, he would walk in the high mountains, in the Himalayas and in the Swiss Alps, so that, he said, his blood would be forced to do its work.

We landed in Paris in the summer. Before I was to go to school, he was keen that I see the city. He called his friend, the architect Rosenthal, who knew the city intimately. Together, he and I would walk and walk. We walked up to Montmartre and visited Le Musée de la Vie Romantique, which had a death mask of my beloved Chopin and a cast of his delicate hand and one of George Sand's arm. We walked the Rive Gauche and stopped at the Café Les Deux Magots, where Simone de Beauvoir and Jean-Paul Sartre discussed existentialism. We walked to Notre Dame and through what had once been the Jewish Ghetto and to Musée Nissim de Camondo, with its impressive collection of Louis XV and Louis XVI furniture, created by a family of Jewish bankers ultimately killed in the Holocaust. We walked to the Père Lachaise cemetery where so many of the world's great men, including J.R.D. Tata and Chopin, lie buried. In those days, there were no maps of the graveyard and we wandered around. I found the painter David's grave quite by chance and so also the grave of the actress Sarah Bernhardt. (They tell me that the grave most frequented is that of

Jim Morrison. *O tempora, o mores*.) We walked to the islands in the Seine, the oldest parts of the city. We went to the Louvre, again and again because there was so much to see there.

I walked Paris and I learnt that to know a city one must walk its streets.

THREE

Of Racists and Other Animals

It was an afternoon of enchantment. The Ecole Communale Publique Suisse let out early on Saturdays and I walked out into the Geneva Street right into the falling snow. It was fresh, white, feathery magic and I wandered down the road, with my seven-year-old nose in the air, watching the snow fall. I had seen snow before. My father had taken me on an eight-hour walk to and from a glacier from Pontresina in the Swiss Alps but there the snow was lying on the ground, grey and without character. This was my first encounter with falling snow. And as I walked, I could tell I was on my way home, for my nose was filled with the familiar scents of the route, the yeasty aroma of fresh bread from the bakery, the sharp scent of fresh flowers at the corner, the heady whiff of chocolate from the chocolatier and next, the sweet smells from the shop of the grocer, my friend . . .

'Run, little one, run,' came a shout. I barely had time to register the voice, that of a senior girl at my school. I turned around and was immediately petrified, the proverbial rabbit in the glare of the headlights. Three louts surrounded me, shouting, 'Look, it's the red fish.'

Did I look like a red fish?

'Let's kill the red fish.'

Kill?

A canvas bag flashed above my head. I fell to the ground.

'How many colours do you have on your body?' one of them shouted. More kicks followed. More blows. I lost consciousness at one point. Oblivion is merciful. I woke up at home. My mother was there and the doctor. They were looking worried. I remember thinking, they shouldn't be worried. I'm safe now. I'm safe here.

It was my first encounter with racism. Over the next few days, I couldn't understand what I had done to upset them so much that they had wanted to hit me with a canvas bag filled with bovver boots. I asked Maman and she tried to explain but her words did not make too much sense.

In retrospect, perhaps I should have seen it coming. Each week, the students would gather in a recreational hall and one of us would be called upon to talk to the others. My teacher, a delicate little thing who would tuck her purple hair into a straw hat with a little straw pompom bobbing on its stalk, once called upon me to talk about the flowers of India.

The next week, she asked if I would speak about the elephant, since that was what most people associated with India. Then there were the festivals of India. Perhaps she was fascinated by India. Perhaps she liked me. Perhaps no one else wanted to speak because the next week, it was again Leela on the cuisine of India.

'Why does your food stink?' someone asked me.

I tried to explain about the spices of India, but even then I was aware that there was one section of the audience that sat stone-faced through my extempore talks.

It was only years later, many years later, that I confronted my demons in London. Hiroji Kubota, the Magnum photographer, was in London and he wanted to shoot the gangs of little boys who had started terrorising the aged in London. Dom was writing the story for the *New York Times Sunday Magazine* and Kubota was photographing it. We traced a gang of three, two of them from one family. They were all heart-breakingly young. The brothers were eight and ten, their friend was eleven. And on a rain-drenched afternoon, they agreed to demonstrate their techniques.

'First we trip 'em,' said one, 'and then we kick 'em wiv our boots.'

I looked down at their boots. There they were. Almost the same kind of boots. I looked up.

'We rip the old buggers,' said his brother. He took a comb from his pocket. It had teeth missing in the middle. He tucked it into one corner of his mouth. 'We cut 'em here. They squeal like pigs.'

He showed me a large raw potato with a razor blade stuck in it. 'Or we cut 'em wiv this.'

When Hiroji was finished, I offered them some sweets.

'Don' want no sweets,' said the leader, 'but yer could stand us a beer.'

Later, we went to meet their parents who didn't seem very concerned about what their children were doing. Perhaps the parents of the young men who had attacked me in Geneva didn't care either. Later, I heard that the family was in distress; the father was missing, the mother, 'sick with alcohol' was in and out of odd jobs and the children were growing up without hope and without dreams. And that is a recipe for a lack of imagination. Violence, to me, is a lack of imagination. You cannot be violent to anyone if you can imagine what it would be like to be in that person's shoes. What those young people in Geneva lacked was also imagination. All they could see was difference and like animals they attacked the different in me, without recognising how much we had in common.

When I recovered, I wanted to go back to school. My father had thought it would be a very good idea for me to go to a public school, where I could mingle with commoner and bourgeois alike. The school authorities were horrified that one of their students should be attacked. They assured Maman that they would take swift action. But they also wondered if I would not be happier in some other less parochial school, a school with a broader base of cosmopolitan students?

My parents had already been planning the move. The attack only accelerated its pace. It was decided that Maman and I would stay in Geneva. Papa would visit on weekends when he could. I went to L'Ecole Rossiaud, a private school for rich Catholic girls where, it was assumed, there would be a greater degree of civilisation and a greater respect for those of other races.

Well, no one attacked me physically but once Abbé Pierre held up Hinduism and India to scorn, it was open season on one Leela Naidu. They surrounded me in the gym, these rich and cosmopolitan Catholic girls, kneeling before me and laughing. They held their sweaty gym shoes up to my nose, asking, 'Is this the way you pray? Is this what you worship?'

Abbé Pierre had no idea of the demons he had let loose with his words. I believe he would have been horrified had he known, but he did not know and I did not tell him. But before it got very bad, I moved again, this time to study at the renowned Ecole Internationale at Geneva. For the next five years, I studied in the English and the French sections simultaneously, and enjoyed myself tremendously. The students were a mixed bag, of course, and among them was Ahmed Khajjar, a pimply-faced youth with a shaggy head of hair, who fell 'madly and extravagantly in love' with me. He was living with his mother who was the exiled queen of the Khajjars of Iran and we took the same tram together to school. Each day, he would be waiting for me, his huge spaniel eyes full of a mournful devotion.

One day, he said he had written a poem for me. I was quite touched until I read the poem: 'Mary had a little lamb . . .' it began.

'I wrote it for you,' he said.

He had only written it out for me but who was I to argue with such an eloquent token of devotion? His mother sent a very polite letter to my mother. It said, in effect, that Ahmed had promised to study better if I would marry him. My mother was startled by this. I was only fourteen at the time and Ahmed probably not very much older, although he was a form behind me in school since he had been detained.

But my mother insisted I go and see her. In the middle of all the paraphernalia of émigré royalty—Persian carpets, antique silverware, drawn curtains—sat Madame la Princesse. She asked me for my hand in marriage for her son. I looked into her world-weary eyes and tried to decide whether she was serious. She seemed to be.

'Madame la Princesse,' I said carefully, 'I cannot marry him but I can try to help him to study.'

I thought it might be a good thing for us to go for a walk in the woods so I could figure out why Ahmed was doing so badly in school. In hindsight that might not have seemed such a great idea—taking a lovesick young man for a walk in the woods—but Ahmed behaved beautifully. He kept telling me dreadful stomach-turning stories about his father and his powers. It seemed his father would cut off the heads of various prisoners and see how long they could run around without their heads. Perhaps he was warning me of the consequences of turning him down.

Finally, I asked him what his problem was with his studies. I knew he wasn't unintelligent.

'I'm not interested,' he said. I tried to reason with him but he stuck to his position. He was not interested so he would not study. A few days later, my mother was reading the newspaper at breakfast. *The Tribune* of Geneva and *Le Monde* both carried stories that Ahmed had died when a private plane crashed. It was sad, I thought, and I hoped that wherever he had gone, he would find something to interest him.

An hour later, the doorbell rang. I went to open it. There stood Ahmed, a look of expectancy on his face. He looked at me and his face crumpled.

'You thought I was dead,' he said, 'and you're not crying.'

He marched past me into the sitting room where my mother looked up, intrigued.

'Oh mon Dieu,' she said. And then, 'Journalism is not what it used to be. The newspapers have it that you have died in a plane crash, Ahmed.'

'You're not crying either,' said Ahmed, even more hurt.

'I should cry because you are alive?' asked my mother, somewhat confused. He had planted the news in the hope that I would discover the error of my ways. I was indeed upset to think of a friend dying but I had not gone into a decline, as Ahmed no doubt hoped.

When I was fifteen years old, I finished at Ecole Internationale and I was to go to Oxford. My father and mother were going back to India so we went to Paris and we began to dismantle our lives. One day as I was walking down the steps that connected the Avenue Camoëns to Avenue Théodore Roosevelt, I saw a familiar but somewhat woeful face.

'Ahmed!' I said.

'Hello, Leela.' he said.

'What are you doing here?' I asked, although I had an inkling that I knew.

We sat together on the steps and I tried to explain that we were too young, that I was going back to India, and no, he couldn't follow, and that he should go back to his mother.

He looked at me, his heart in his eyes.

'Oh Ahmed,' I said, 'all you need to do is find out what you want to do. If you don't want to study, don't. But find something you want to do and you will do it.'

Then I left him, sitting on the steps. Many years later, I discovered that he had moved back to Iran and become one of the finest documentary filmmakers there. He named his daughter Leela. It is a compliment I treasure.

~

'L'Ecole Int' as we all learnt to call it had a system of mentoring for new students. When I joined, it was deemed that I did not need a 'pilot' because I had come to Geneva before, I spoke French, I knew my way around, I had been '*acclimatisée*'. But then Virginia, a Jewish girl whose father was a British businessman, arrived and I was given charge of her. According to the tradition of the school, she was meant to invite me to her home for dinner at the end of three months, as a token of her gratitude, I suppose. And so one evening a blue Cadillac drew up outside our home and I was whisked off to dinner in a penthouse apartment with a view of Lake Geneva.

Unfortunately, it did not seem that the family was accustomed to money. Virginia was not interested in the view or in the historic city with its great concerts, operas, ballets, and theatre in several languages. She lived with her grandmother and the old lady wanted to show me how the cupboards lit up when they were opened. I exclaimed dutifully over the illuminated interiors. Should one need to dress in the middle of the night, what a blessing that would be, to have a cupboard with a built-in light. Of course, one could put on the bedroom lights too, but to mention this would be to deny the old lady her joy so I tried to look interested. But when she kept opening and shutting the cupboard doors, I am afraid my appreciation began to get a little mechanical.

We sat down to dinner, the three of us in a huge room, served by a butler. The napery was damask, the cutlery was sterling silver but the food was unimaginative and indifferent. Of course, there was caviar. It was then the ultimate status symbol. Virginia insisted on Melba toast and she insisted that hers be buttered on both sides. She daubed huge amounts of caviar on the toast. And then a chicken stew arrived in a white flour sauce. It was pure stodge, but then the trifle that rounded off the meal was sweet stodge.

'And now,' announced Virginia, 'I am going to show you my father's office.'

'Ooh!' I thought to myself. 'Will I be able to control my delight?'

We went into an office that looked as if it had been wheeled off a Hollywood set. There was a huge desk and armchairs and books by the yard and heavy drapes.

And on the table, there was a lamp.

The shade was the colour of old parchment.

'What do you think that is made of?' asked Virginia. I had no idea but I was sure she was going to tell me.

'Human skin,' she said triumphantly.

I looked at her, disbelieving.

'It's from Auschwitz,' she said.

My disbelief grew.

'You don't believe me?' she asked. 'Look.'

She turned the lamp slowly. On one side, there was a number. It was a number they tattooed on the arm of each person who entered a concentration camp like Auschwitz.

I felt my gorge rise. I turned and I ran, right out of that penthouse, out into the street and home. I threw myself at my mother and wept in her lap until I felt slightly better. I was glad that I did not need to talk to Virginia again.

~

But of course, that did not mean I could purge racists from my life, not even when I was the daughter-in-law of a rich family that had every comfort at its command. They were always there, hovering in the background, dreadful people who let unimportant matters—such as the creed into which you were born or the colour of your skin or the shape of your nose—determine their responses to you.

At the time, I was still married to Tikki Oberoi and we were travelling en famille in America. One evening in Washington, Rai Bahadur Oberoi announced that he would like to go to a self-service cafeteria to see how the system worked. The next morning, Rai Bahadur, my mother-in-law, Tikki and I left the hotel in which we were staying and set out to find a cafeteria. We had breakfast there but only after the Rai Bahadur had satisfied his curiosity about how the orders were processed and how everything was kept moving.

When we finished, I went out to find us a taxi. A taxi pulled over and parked at the kerb. I explained to the rather elderly driver that we would have to wait a few moments until the other passengers came out of the cafeteria. He was very polite about it.

Just then a huge car came barrelling around the corner and scraped the taxi. Then the driver stood on his brakes, stopped with a screech of rubber and jumped out of his car. He was a large white man. He took a look at the taxi driver who happened to be black and began to heap the most frightful racist abuse on him. In between, he assured the driver that he would make sure he was sacked, that the driver was one of those people who should be.

I couldn't bear it. I stepped around the car and said in as cold a tone as I could manage while still being polite. 'Excuse me, but I saw what happened. The taxi was stationary. You were in motion. You are at fault. And if you insist on taking this further, I will be glad to be a witness.'

Unfortunately, we were leaving the next day for India. So I wrote down my version of events and signed it. Then I gave the driver my address and told him that I would be willing to answer any questions that either insurance company might have. A few days later, I did get a questionnaire that the insurance company wanted me to fill out. I filled it out and sent it back.

And a few weeks later, I got a letter of thanks from the driver. I didn't need to be thanked. I was glad to do what I could. After all, I was no stranger to racism. I spent a good part of my life in India, home to any number of racisms. It is not enough that we have a caste system which has brutalised both upper and lower castes for centuries, oh no. India has other racisms as well. One of our most important values is how much melanin your skin has.

When Dom and I began work on his population book, *A Matter of People*, one of our first stops was Calcutta. There we were to meet Mother Teresa, apostle of the poor, saint of the slums and the woman who had used every weapon in her power, including her considerable charisma, to keep the Catholics from using contraception.

Dom took a dim view of this but I thought she was just a Roman Catholic nun, part of the hierarchies of the Vatican, and subject to its diktats. When we met, their dislike was instantaneous and mutual.

'Come and pray with me,' she said. Dom refused to do any such thing. I went with her into a spartan chapel with a cement floor on which she kneeled to pray. We prayed together and Dom paced the floor on the veranda outside.

Then she came out and said, 'You go. Leave Leela with me.'

'Certainly not,' Dom snorted. Not unsurprisingly, she did not find mention in *A Matter of People*. But I thought Dom had allowed his personal animus to get in the way of quite an interesting story.

When the Vatican finally agreed that to use the rhythm method was not a mortal sin, when it was finally agreed that women should do complicated sums, Mother Teresa's volunteers went out to help the poor and the downtrodden Catholics of Crematorium Street understand the method. It is not an easy method. It uses the menstrual cycle to predict the woman's most fertile time of the month—that is when she is most likely to become pregnant. Once she has identified her fertile time, she is supposed to abstain during that period.

Since many of them were illiterate women, the Church had decided that the best way to teach them would be to give them bead necklaces of different colours. They were supposed to string the beads using different coloured beads for fertile days and for other days. Mrs Lovejoy—and the other volunteers like her who fanned out into the slums, including the biggest one at Pilkhana—was supposed to distribute these necklaces and make sure that they were used. And yet everywhere we could see evidence that it was a method that was failing. There were many children in every home and many of these were ill-fed and hungry. In other homes, the necklaces had broken and the different coloured beads had been restrung haphazardly. In some homes, the children were playing with the beads. Some women kept their beads in their little puja niches behind their clay images of the Devi and simply hoped that she would do their counting for them. And the children continued to be born.

Mother Teresa's Missionaries of Charity did not seem to be living up to their name in their treatment of Mrs Lovejoy. She received a bag of wheat flour (which I estimated would contain about five kilos of flour), a kilo of sugar, a packet of tea and some kerosene oil every month. There was no milk, no rice and no vegetables. She was also given a stipend of Rs 200 a month, which was not sufficient to feed and clothe herself, her unemployed husband and their five children. To pay so little to a woman who was a qualified nurse seemed to me to be absurd but Mrs Lovejoy of Crematorium Street kept on working. She defined commitment and she never complained.

I was amazed at her resilience, at her courage and at her persistence. So we invited her and her family to dinner. The family ate circumspectly since Mrs Lovejoy made sure she ordered enough but not too much, but I could see that the little ones were almost getting drunk on the food. She told us that she would like another job. I thought she would do well as a housekeeper in the Park Hotel in which we were staying so I talked to the manager about her.

He agreed that she seemed to be the perfect fit and he also said that he had a vacancy for a housekeeper. Then he asked to meet her. I knew her sincerity and her simplicity would impress him. But when I asked him what happened, he said, 'Madam, we could not hire her.'

'Why not?' I asked.

'Madam, we thought with a name like Lovejoy, she would be fair.'

'Fair?'

'Yes, like an Anglo-Indian. But she was too dark.'

Before we accuse other nations of racism, we should examine our own consciences. In a way, caste is another terrible form of racism. This was brought home to me one day in Delhi, when I found my domestic help, Anguri, weeping.

I waited until the tears had abated and then asked what the matter was. She told me that she lived by the banks of the Yamuna, in what was then called a Harijan settlement. They had bought the land at a public auction held by the Indian Railways, collecting the money by selling almost everything they had, pawning their jewellery and even—and this for the poor is a terrible sacrifice—selling their goats. They had managed to buy it because no one else wanted it. It was seen as unusable land, *usar* land. But over the years, they had cleared it, removing pebbles and stones by hand, mixing dung and compost waste into it, so that now it was ready for the humble ragi (millet) crop with which they hoped to feed themselves.

And as soon as the land was arable, another group had moved in, with tractors and buffalos. The animals would graze on the young plants and the tractors would finish what was left. The police were in cahoots with this group, and every time the Harijans protested, the police moved in. They would arrest the men and throw them into gaol for nine days, declaring their scythes as weapons. The women would get six days. This meant a further loss of labour wages while their fields were being ravaged.

'Tell me when they come next,' I said.

But first I needed to understand what was going on, so I called our friend, Jag Parvesh Chandra, a man who knew more about Delhi and its communities than most people had forgotten.

'This must be an upper-caste group,' he said. 'It's almost always a caste issue.'

One evening Anguri told me that the men had threatened to return under cover of night.

'How do I get there?' I asked.

She was aghast. 'Bibiji, please don't come. You don't know these men. They can do anything. They have guns.'

I thought she was exaggerating. Later that night, I took a cab and counted three bridges.

'There is no path down from the bridge, bibiji. You will have to clamber down or slip and slide down,' Anguri had said. I could see that she was right.

From the bridge I could see four tractors. I asked the cab to wait and raced down the slope.

'Who are you?' I thundered at them.

There was a surprised male rumble from behind the lights of the tractors. As my eyes got used to the light, I could see that the men were indeed carrying rifles. I do not remember fear. I only remember my outrage.

'This is not your land. These people have bought it from the government and they have tended it. You will go back now.'

There was some surprise at this but not enough. I needed to turn on some big guns. I put on my best 'maharani manner' and announced that I was going to make a full report to the tahsildar of the Railways and to Mrs Indira Gandhi who was a personal friend.

When the tractors began to back off, I heard another car draw up on the bridge.

'Leela?' I could hear Dom's voice. 'Is that you?'

'Down here,' I shouted.

Dom made the cab driver help him down the slope and he arrived cursing and swearing at the bottom. 'What are you doing here?' he asked.

I explained. He looked like his question had not been answered.

The next day, I sat down and wrote a long letter to Mrs Gandhi. Whatever her faults, she was not slow to take decisions. The next day I was notified by the PMO, the prime minister's office, that I was to go with the tahsildar of the Railways and identify land for a new settlement.

And so one Leela Naidu and one tahsildar went off with some land records, chugging along in an inspection wagon. This was basically a bench on wheels that could seat four. It had a back, a seat and the arms ran out in front and behind as handles that six men, three on either side, were pushing. On this contraption, we went chugging into Uttar Pradesh, looking for likely land.

At one point, a bunch of men leapt out of the fields where they had been waiting for us. They were armed with sticks. The tahsildar made a dash for it and hid behind a bush. I drew myself up to my full height and said, 'Yesterday, they had guns and I survived. You have brought sticks? Tahsildar saahab?'

The tahsildar came out, looking sheepish.

The sight of a government official dispersed them and we trundled along again until we came across a decapitated body across the tracks. The tahsildar clucked a bit. He wanted the body moved so that we could continue our odd journey and get it over with. But I was having none of it.

'Find his head,' I said. 'And find out who he is.' The men looked a bit put out.

I got out of our wheelbarrow. 'I am not going anywhere unless you find his head, reunite it with his body and go and find out who he was and make sure his parents or his family know.'

It took some doing but finally, some dignity had been accorded to the dead. Then the tahsildar showed me a piece of land, crawling with mosquitoes, filled with rocks and pebbles. I did write another letter but I don't think it worked. I believe the settlement was relocated and the matter ended there.

I tried but when you have thousands of years of prejudice on one side and an economically backward community on the other, it is not difficult to guess which side wins all the time.

~

Finally there was my run-in with those who practise a religion in its outward form but ignore its basic principles. And whatever theologians may say or priests may opine, the basic principle of every religion enjoins upon us an admission of our common humanity, and a respect that should grow out of it.

It was a hot day in April 1983 and a Friday. Across the street from where I live is a building called Allana House, which has a mosque in its garage. Every Friday, namaaz was offered at this mosque and the road was blocked to traffic as the faithful gathered to pray on the road.

But this was no ordinary Friday. I was going to bring my father home from Bombay Hospital where he had been recovering from a stroke. Dom offered to come with me, and to this day, I have never been able to decide whether this was one of those incidental kindnesses or it was an intuition. Before we set out, I went down to talk to the young men in charge of setting up the barricades and blocking the traffic. I explained that I was bringing an old man, a sick old man home and that I would need to be able to bring the taxi up to the gate of the building. I explained that he would not have the strength to climb even a few stairs. They assured me that it would be all right, that the barricades would not stretch the entire length of the road.

But when we returned home, Dom in the front seat of the taxi and my father in the back seat with me, we found that the road had been three-quarters blocked, leaving no room for a car to pass. I got down from the cab and approached the barricades. It was around noon and the sun was beating down on our heads. I waited for the prayer to finish and then I asked the men at the barricades whether I could get the taxi in. I explained that it was an old man, a sick man . . . but the whole lot ignored me. I might have been a cockroach for all anyone cared.

The Koran speaks beautifully of the milk of human kindness. It speaks of respect for all life. It does not suggest that one should ignore the old and the infirm. I felt an anger rise in me. These men could not be praying. They could not be reaching out towards something larger than themselves if what they were doing allowed them to ignore the needs of an old man.

Finally, my patience ran out. 'Are you praying or performing gymnastics?' I asked.

This was enough to set them off. Two hefty butchers, clad in the lungis of their trade, leapt at me. One of them spat in my eyes, blurring my vision with a gobbet of thick phlegm. Then both of them grabbed me by the arms, lifting me off the ground, while one of them hit me on the head and the other punched me in the kidneys. Others went for the taxi, climbing on to it and thumping at the roof. There was rage in their voices as they threatened to burn the taxi, and kill whoever was inside it. The taxi driver fled, leaving his keys in the car.

I do not know whether we would have survived this onslaught but help was at hand. Mrs Lucia Gurung, whose home on Mereweather Street allowed her a view of our proceedings, came to her balcony to see what was going on. She sent her nephew off to get the police. He happened on a traffic police officer in his open black jeep and brought him to the scene. As soon as they saw a uniform, the brave young men who were beating a woman and trying to terrorise an old man, began to run.

The traffic policeman got the taxi towed up to the building. He got us all up two floors, taking my father first, carrying him in a football tackle. The air was still full of violence and threats. 'The old man doesn't go anywhere, but the woman should watch her step,' an anonymous male voice shouted. 'We'll burn the building down,' shouted another. 'The husband. The husband, he has to come out. A quick slash with a knife . . .'

I got my father settled and Dom into bed. Dom had been roughed up; they had taken off their footwear and hit him in the face, an offence that offered more psychological hurt than physical harm, but they had broken his spectacles too. Then Mrs Gurung and Dr Navin Kumar, both of whom were active in the South Mumbai community of Colaba, came to see us. I was in growing pain but I had not had time for tears.

'You must make a police complaint,' said Mrs Gurung.

I went with them to the police station. There sat a constable with a stub of pencil behind his ear and the air of a man who was not likely to be surprised by anything in the world.

I explained that a mob had attacked me.

'Mr Mob or Mrs Mob?' he asked in Bambaiya Hindi. I had the distinct impression that I had stepped through the looking glass.

Then a young man was brought into the police station. Not a yard from where I was sitting, a policeman began to beat him brutally, slapping his face, dragging him up when he slumped, slapping him again and again.

I could not take it any more. I walked away but I was in tears.

Later when K.A. Abbas heard of what had happened, he wrote a very public apology. He knew that I had read the Koran in Devnagari and that I was a Sufi. I would not have offered disrespect to any religion. His legendary column that took the back page of the *Blitz* had the headline 'Leela, Forgive Us'.

~

But I want also to say that humanity is not always like that. I met my dearest friend in Geneva, the same city in which I was attacked. She was Catherine Lombard then, she is Catherine Kuhn-Lombard now. I was Leela Naidu then, and I am Leela Naidu-Moraes now. Our friendship has lasted fifty-seven years, since the time we met as girls, and it has survived a trip we made together to south India when we were both in our fifties. I have been told that travelling together may be fatal to a friendship, but I remember Catherine leaning out of a window and turning into a schoolgirl again with excitement.

'Leela, Leela,' she shouted, 'the cows are yellow!'

It was, of course, a turmeric bath for the family cow, a white one, on an auspicious day in Kerala. But we laughed together as we leaned out of the windows of our hotel, laughed as if we were schoolgirls again, munching Toblerone and bread as we walked through another landscape, which we absorbed with younger eyes.

FOUR

Another Home

We returned to India in 1955, when Daddy had been transferred to Delhi as the Science Director for UNESCO, South-East Asia. He had known Kamaladevi Chattopadhyaya, the Gandhian freedom fighter and patron of the arts, for years and when she heard that we had returned, she invited all of us to her home in Electric Lane for a performance by Balasaraswati, one of the greatest bharatanatyam dancers of any age.

I was wearing a Kanjeevaram sari and sitting with my parents, when I was politely summoned 'backstage' by Balu, who was both her brother and her *nattuvanar*, the one who keeps time and calls out the *jathi*s.

I was now in the presence of the legendary Balasaraswati in her makeshift green room, where she was waiting for me.

'I want your petticoat tape,' she said when I had made my namaskaaram.

I goggled a bit at that. How would *my* sari stay up?

'I will tie up your petticoat with a knot,' she said.

And so I gave up my petticoat tape and she tied a knot in my petticoat. Then I draped my sari back around myself. Next, I was ordered to get a hibiscus for her hair. Holding on to my sari, I tottered off to pluck a flower. (I need not have worried. The knot was so secure that it took both my mother and me to work it loose at the end of the evening.)

But when she began to dance, I forgot all about this. She was dancing on a veranda, lit only by a stand of many diyas, perfectly positioned so that it would throw her shadow on to the wall of the house. She was by then a mature woman, full of figure, her arms like hams. But in front of our eyes, she became a beautiful young Radha, pining for her Krishna. Her body was her instrument.

The next day we went to the Vigyan Bhavan for a seminar on dance. There was Rukminidevi Arundale who gave a talk in which she described how bharatanatyam had not been considered a respectable form until she came along. Then Mrinalini Sarabhai spoke and she said that bharatanatyam had not been a respectable form until she came along.

I wondered whether Mesdames Arundale and Sarabhai had thought about what they were saying, about the effect it would have on a woman who had actually started out her life expecting to be a devadasi or temple dancer. But Balasaraswati's expressive face—her *abhinaya* was legendary—was impassive.

Then it was her turn to address the audience. She said that she would not speak. She would dance. And in a corner of that stage, without proper lighting, without proper accompaniment, she danced spontaneously, beautifully, singing as she danced and once again she became Krishna, before our eyes, Krishna who was saving the world from the net of Maya.

When she had finished, we were leaving. I was wrapped up in what I had seen, eager to go home and replay it all, to process it and understand it or at least get a sense of it, when a loud carrying voice stopped all of us in our tracks.

'Naidu gaaru,' called Balasaraswati.

We stopped and turned.

'My mother was a devadasi in your temple,' she said. 'Now your daughter Leela—she will be a dancer. Balu will come to your home tomorrow and I will come with him.'

My mother was delighted and wanted to know if there was anything special she would like to eat.

'Lots of sweets,' said the dancer. Of course, she was diabetic and of course, she ignored the advice that her doctors gave her.

The next day she came around teatime. She tucked into the sweets and told me the story of her life.

'My mother was my first guru. Then she sent me to Kittappa Pillai. He would hit me with a plank with nails embedded in it wherever my posture was not correct. I took that for a while and then I ran away and went back to my mother. I told her that I wouldn't dance and I didn't. I didn't dance for five years.'

I could completely sympathise with a little girl who . . .

'But I missed it and one day I told her I would dance again but only if he would not hit me.'

And so began my first lessons in bharatanatyam with a woman who straddled two eras: the one in which it was seen as a debased temple form danced by devadasis and the other in which it had become a classical art form meant for middle-class girls and performed in front of admiring audiences across the world.

In the next three weeks that Balu was in Delhi, he came every day and gave me a basic grounding in bharatanatyam. Then he got his marching orders and had to leave for Chennai. Those three magical weeks had only whetted my appetite. I had not learnt either ballet or modern dance in order to perform. I was not intent on learning bharatanatyam in order to present my skills at an arangetram. But if I was finally to live in India, I felt I would be able to understand my country just that much more if I knew the rhythms of its dances.

Daddy had known sitarist Ravi Shankar in Paris when he would come there as a child, accompanying his brother Uday Shankar on the latter's tours. He would come to meet my parents whenever he was in Delhi. When he heard that I was interested in dance, he sent Debuda, the third brother, to teach me dancing. That was an entirely different experience. Where Balasaraswati had concentrated on tradition and found freedom to express herself within that tradition, Debu was a syncretist at heart. When he was sure that my body was obeying the ancient geometry of bharatanatyam—the straight line between the shoulder blade and the elbow, the square formed by the thighs in a squatting position with the knees in a vertical line with the feet—we began to incorporate elements of Odissi and Bengali folk dance forms. We would even improvise a little from time to time.

I wondered, of course, whether I should try and get into an Indian college before going to Oxford. To that end, my batch-mate at L'Ecole Internationale, Kay Myrdal, the daughter of Gunnar Myrdal, the economist, and I went to meet the principal at Miranda House. I tried to prime Kay before we went in.

'They will ask us some fairly loopy questions.'

'Loopy? Let them try,' laughed Kay.

My heart sank. She thought they were going to test us. I rather thought that the only test would be our patience. And so it was.

We were ushered into the room of the man who was supposed to interview us and decide whether we were suitable for Miranda House. He may have been some kind of vice-principal. I cannot remember. I have always been bad with bureaucracies. I don't even remember his name. I have always been bad with the names of people whom I do not like.

'Do you know how to use a dictionary?' he asked.

Kay began to splutter. Applying a firm but gentle pressure to her ankle, I assured him we did.

'Do you know how to read a map?' he asked.

'*Calmes toi*,' I said to Kay, hoping that she would heed my advice and stay calm. Then I said to the man, 'Yes, we can.'

'Do you read the papers?' he asked.

I did not dare look at Kay but I knew she would be red in the face.

'We do,' I said.

'You know why I am asking you?' he asked.

'We don't,' I said.

'Because when you read a word in the papers that you do not understand, you can look up the dictionary. And if you see a news article about a place you do not know, you can find it on the map.'

Kay got up suddenly. There was a moment when I feared that she would explode. But she didn't.

'Come, Leela,' she said.

We left together and that put paid to the notion of my joining a college in India. I would wait and go to Oxford, I thought. At that point, I had no idea that a few years later, I would be playing a dancer in my first film. But then I also had no idea that I was to be married to Tilak Raj Oberoi, bear twins, go through a divorce, lose my daughters thanks to the regressive stance of the Hindu Marriage Act, which granted the male parent custody as a matter of course, and start acting before I was twenty years old.

But oddly, my preparation for a career in cinema started when I went to Paris to see a doctor.

FIVE

Paris by Renoir

'Meet my daughter Leela,' my father began to say when I was pregnant. 'It takes you a few minutes to walk around her.'

But then that was my father's way. Dilip Kumar (his real name was Yusuf) was a friend and we went to see *Ganga Jumna* with him. In the course of the film, my father heard a phrase, 'ullu ka patta'.

'What does that mean?' he asked Yusuf saahab.

'It means, "son of an owl".'

'Can I call my daughter "ullu ki patti"?' he asked.

Yusuf saahab looked a little surprised but he considered it in his logical fashion. Then he delivered his verdict. 'I suppose so,' he said and I got a new nickname.

I had always been slim and I was carrying the twins in the front. After I delivered them, I began to have some problems with the muscles of my lower abdomen. They had been distended so far that they weren't recovering normally. At that time Roberto Rossellini was in India. He enjoyed my mother's cooking and my father's conversation and would often drop in at Sujan Singh Park in Delhi where they lived.

'Ingrid had the same problems after she had the twins,' he told my parents. 'She went to Dr Samoil. Send Leela to him.'

The only problem was that Dr Samoil was in Paris. I wonder if anyone would believe what we had to go through to go abroad in those days. I was going on 'medical grounds' but the government wanted a government hospital to certify you as sick. So Daddy and I went off to a hospital where a woman with a moustache put me on a gurney.

'Lift your legs,' she said.

Dr Thomas, the British surgeon who delivered my twins, said that he should have put me in a steel corset but what saved me was the ballet training. It was not that I did not want to raise my legs, but my muscles were so weak that I could not. I hated the idea of being helpless. I hated the idea of inhabiting a body that would not obey me. So when she asked me to lift my legs, I tried. The moustachio-ed doctor may have thought I was malingering but when she saw the strain on my face, she was moved to help. Together we got my legs up, but then I found I couldn't even lower them again.

She came out of the examination room and looked at my father. 'I think she has a medical problem,' she said to him.

'We think so too,' said my father dryly and my passport was duly stamped.

But I went to Paris and called Ingrid Bergman, not without a butterfly or two fluttering weakly in my weakened stomach. 'Ingrid *est un peu cabotin*,' said her husband. That was a nasty word, an almost untranslatable word. It meant that she was a grandstander, someone who acted from the surface but not from within. I didn't think so but I kept my opinion to myself. I did not think I knew enough to argue with Rossellini but I also felt a little as though I had let my own opinions down.

The voice on the other end of the telephone line was warm, welcoming and I presented myself and my letter of introduction to Ingrid Bergman who was at the Hotel Rafael. With her were a round little man with a pug nose and the pink cheeks of a Provencal farmer and a petite woman with a tight-lipped expression.

'You are an actress,' said the round little man. The tight-lipped woman continued to look tight-lipped.

This was not the first time I had been told who I was or would be. Mulk Raj Anand, who was also a friend of my father, had told me that I would be an actress. I remember being a bit appalled at the thought. It seemed like a limiting definition when there was so much that I thought I could be. But the round little man had an engaging way with him and I was older so I explained that I was not an actress. I added that I had done some amateur theatre at school in Geneva, but he simply shrugged.

'You are an actress,' he repeated.

That was when Ingrid suddenly saw fit to introduce all of us.

'This is Leela from India,' she said. 'And this is Jean Renoir and his wife Dido.'

This was the Renoir whom the hot heads of the New Wave cinema acknowledged as the maestro. This was the Renoir who had come to India to make *The River*, a film I had seen and loved, the film on which Satyajit Ray had assisted Renoir and come into contact with the practice of Neo-realism.

Renoir was working on a play with Bergman, a French version of Robert Anderson's *Tea and Sympathy*. A retrospective of his films had been organised by the Cinémathèque de Paris and he insisted I come with him and his wife, Dido, the imposing woman who had until then sat looking at me without any expression. She turned out to be a warm and wonderful person who took me under her wing a bit.

~

Dr Samoil's treatment consisted of injections of hormones from live chickens and a strict diet. I was allowed only watercress, cheese and Ryvita crackers. I didn't really mind too much although it could get a little boring so I made up for it by getting myself a table by the window and watching the parade of life swinging by me in the dining room of the Hotel Meurice. Not that I was being unduly curious. Oh never mind, I was being unduly curious, but if you have ever lived for weeks on a certain limited diet, you will find that you need distraction too.

France is one of the few countries where they allow you to bring your pet into a restaurant with you. This meant that many of the ladies who lunched there, lunched with their pet pooches. Did they, I wonder, choose their dogs for the resemblance? Or did they simply grow to resemble the beings they loved most? For these ladies were devoted to their dogs. One would come in, every Thursday, and bring her dog with her. They would dine together and the dog would drink his soup out of a silver bowl. One day, Fido did not want his nice potage.

The woman went berserk. She called for the waiter. She demanded to see the manager. She ordered the chef into her presence. 'My dog is not eating his soup,' she shrieked. 'Something must be wrong with it.'

The chef drew himself up to his full height. 'Perhaps,' he said with a huge dose of Gallic contempt, 'perhaps it would be best for him to eat at some other establishment.'

A chill fell over the dining room. The woman swept out, her dog by her side. I thought Fido looked a little embarrassed. Whoever she was, the woman must have been accustomed to throwing her name around and getting things done. I could never bear that kind of person.

I must have been around thirteen at the time when I visited Eden Rock at Cap d'Antibes. It was an awfully elegant place, and it kept the hoi polloi out not just with its high gates but also by an almost indefinable air of privilege that it exuded. Perhaps it was because every one of the wait staff wore impeccable white gloves or because of the guest book which seemed like a roll call of the rich, the famous and the bejewelled.

Maman and I were there at the invitation of my 'fairy queen', the beautiful Princess Niloufer of Hyderabad, who had a lovely lazy voice and gorgeous red hair. She was married to the euphoniously named Mufakkam Jha. He once asked me to kiss him but even as a little girl, I was having none of that.

'I have indigestion,' I squeaked, 'You will get it too.' Under cover of the laughter, I made my escape.

At Eden Rock, they produced the Guest Book. 'Perhaps her highness would like to sign it?' the manager cooed.

Her highness? I noticed a naughty glint in the eye of Princess Niloufer. She had obviously told them that I was also royalty. So in my best copperplate, I inscribed a suitable remark and signed myself as Leela, the Princess of Kuchh-Nahin!

But I could see why the world was fascinated with royalty. When the King of Spain was having lunch at the restaurant of the Meurice, I watched with fascination as eight large rainbow trout were taken to the table. By then I was fairly well acquainted with the staff and so I allowed myself the luxury of a little vulgar curiosity.

'Eight trout?' I asked Monsieur Jacques, the maître d', a stately presence.

'He only eats the cheeks,' he said.

It seemed a little wasteful, I thought, as I addressed myself once again to my watercress and hard cheese.

But it would have been all hard cheese for me, had I not been adopted by the Renoirs. He asked me to select a play so that we could read a scene together. I chose Anouilh's *La Sauvage*, which dealt with Thérèse, a young gypsy girl who could play the violin beautifully. She falls in love with Florent, a rich young man, whom Anouilh refers to as *l'enfant doré*, the golden young man. In the end, when she is about to be dressed to wed this man, she takes off the dress and walks away. It was this scene that I had chosen to read.

I arrived at his home right on time. I was let into the house by his housekeeper who told me to go into his study. A fire hissed in the fireplace and before it sat Jean Renoir and Paul Meurisse, an actor of the Comédie Française, whom I knew by reputation and by his work in Clouzot's *Les Diaboliques*. I reminded myself that I knew nervousness was simply a waste of energy. I reminded myself that these were human beings like me. I reminded myself that I was only an amateur actress who was being given the unique opportunity to work with two of the great talents of French performing arts. I reminded myself of all that, but underneath it ran: Meurisse-Renoir, Renoir-Meurisse, Meurisse-Renoir.

The only thing to do then was to step into La Sauvage's shoes and ignore Leela Naidu and her fear of failure. And so it began, a delightful reading of a single scene. For a while Meurisse read Florent, leading me beautifully, opening up spaces for me, allowing me to feel my way into the scene. Some actors want to diminish you; but the truly great ones are generous enough to enhance you. Meurisse was like that. He had to leave eventually for a rehearsal and Renoir and I continued. He led me through a series of exercises in what he described as the 'ifness' of the play. If Thérèse were only a competent violinist and not a superb one, how would she react? If Thérèse were not a gypsy but a middle-class girl, how would she react? What would her reasons be for leaving Florent then? What if her parents had behaved themselves? Each time, I modified my performance and each time I was pushed a little further in my understanding of acting. How would her body language change if she had been beaten by Florent? What if her leaving was an act of inverted snobbery? Let us introduce here, *ma petite* Leela, a note of hubris. Let us say, her walking away from Florent, through those French windows, is an act of the ego. Now, let us assume your set has no French windows. How does she leave?

It was exhausting and it was exhilarating but at the end of it, Renoir looked as if he were ready for more.

Then he said something that I have treasured all my life, wisdom from the master, as it were: 'You do not need to go to any school for acting. Acting comes from within. You can work it all out from within, as long as you have enough within. Think it out on your own, but think it out from A to Z.'

As I left, he walked me out of the house. In the garden was his head in bronze.

'Is that by your father?' I asked.

'Could I afford something my father had sculpted or painted?' he laughed.

The next day, Renoir took me to meet his agents, Musical Corporation of America (MCA). He was clear in his instructions.

'You must make a dossier for Leela,' he said. This is not half as exciting as it sounds, since it only means a file. 'She has thin skin so no heavy make-up when you take her photographs. It will also reflect light so no dramatic lighting. She must not be used as an exotic. She can do anything for the camera and the stage. But she cannot play a prostitute or a criminal or someone caught in the middle of a war. She is far too sensitive for that.'

They scribbled all of it down and I began to wonder what was happening. But Renoir left no time for that. 'I refuse to be bored,' he once said to me. It seemed to be his way of addressing life, with a wide-eyed wonder, a decision to be interested, to find something that would hold him.

As I said, Dido and he adopted me. We went to see his Paris retrospective, a veritable treasure trove of cinema, together. Renoir was not much of a party person, but he would consent to go out to dinner if he thought the people might amuse him. He only accepted dinner invitations if he thought he would not be bored by the company. At one dinner party thrown by M D'Assault, a very cultivated man, I was seated across the table from Maurice Chevalier who was in sparklingly good form. At some point, we were all taken to the pantry to see a much-prized mynah bird which M D'Assault assured us could read the Bible.

As we walked down a dark corridor, we could hear a very human voice shouting imprecations.

'Idiot, fool,' the voice shouted irritably. 'Put on the light.' As we turned the corner, the idiot who had obeyed this peremptory command was revealed. It was a Persian blue, a cat that is not known for its docility or its obedience. But this was we discovered a very special mynah bird, and it had a will to power.

Alberto Sardi, the Italian comic actor, tried to flatter it but in vain. His overtures were returned with a volley of abuse that a sailor would have been proud to claim for his own. One of the gorgeous and effete young men in Louis Quatorze outfits, who were serving us at table, one behind each guest, tried to quell it by covering it with a red velvet drape. The mynah was having none of that and began to abuse again. Like Goethe, it wanted more light. Finally, we returned to our table and I found myself talking to Louise de Vilmorin who had some very perceptive remarks to make about India.

Rossellini had also provided me with a letter of introduction to the *Cahiers du Cinema*. I went to their office and almost at once, I was chatting to François Truffaut. The letter did its work and on the days that I was not with Renoir and Dido, I was going to see great films, and the films of James Dean. (For some reason, the French were obsessed with his films. But then it seems that they have an inability to deal with America and its popular culture in any sensible manner; witness their love of James Hadley Chase!) After the film, we would go to a café and discuss it. I would listen to Truffaut protesting the use of artificial lighting or Jean-Luc Godard analysing a shot.

One late evening, we were driving back across le Pont des Beaux Arts in a taxi. The air was thick with the smoke of several conversations and Gauloises going simultaneously. As we crossed the river, I heard a cry, '*Au secours, au secours.*'

I stopped the cab and we all spilt out on to the bridge. There in the murky water of the Seine was an enormous woman. Neither Godard nor Truffaut could swim but we had two other energetic young men with us. Despite the bitter winter night, they stripped and jumped in. We rushed off to get an ambulance and finally, the woman was dragged ashore. She was obviously very drunk. As soon as the water had been pumped out of her lungs, she looked around and realised that she had quite an audience. Truffaut and Godard were looking down at her bemused. Then there were her rescuers who were being given shots of brandy and were huddling in blankets. Along with the ambulance attendants and a couple of stragglers, it was quite a respectable audience and the diva in her rose to the surface again.

'Oh, let me die,' she moaned. 'Why did you not let me die?'

This was more than her rescuers, shivering in the cold, could bear. 'Shut up,' said one of them. 'Or we will throw you back in.' She shut up and we went home.

I could not think of any way of repaying Renoir for all that he had done for me so I settled for a gesture. I planned a meal at the Hotel Meurice. I did not think myself sufficiently entertaining and so I planned to invite Ingrid Bergman and Truffaut and Goddard as well. Le grand chef, summoned by Monsieur Jacques, was unimpressed by their names but M Renoir? It was a name to reckon with. M le Chef was thrown into paroxysms of delight at the thought of being challenged to please such a demanding palate. M le Chef knew that M Renoir was a gourmet and he, himself—M le Chef—knew exactly what M Renoir liked. He was not one of those American idiots who insisted on lobster with café au lait. For M Renoir, l'homard, oui, mais à l'Armoricaine with the finest asparagus and artichoke hearts and salads. There would be crêpes Suzette flambé for dessert and with it, white wine and champagne.

Should you ever have lunch with such a guest-list, go up to your room and make notes as soon as it is over. The bon mots you think you will remember for the rest of your life will pass into oblivion. The elegant repartee will fade. The heady badinage will be lost in the millions of other trivial words you will hear. You will kick yourself if you don't make notes.

Excuse me while I kick myself.

~

Ingrid was blessed with a rather peculiar sense of humour. By this time Rossellini was already in the middle of his Indian affair with Sonali Dasgupta. The Parisian press was abuzz with rumours about this and suddenly, I was in their midst, a young Indian woman . . .

And so Ingrid invited me to lunch at Maxim's. She seemed to be sure we would be photographed and so we were. (After all, she was an international star.) The next morning, I appeared in the papers, at Maxim's, under the name of Sonali Dasgupta.

Ingrid rang me up with her signature deep chuckle. 'They are such fools,' she said but there was a savage edge to her voice.

On the day of the premiere of *Tea and Sympathy*, Renoir called at the hotel. I had not assumed that I would be invited to it but I was thrilled. 'Wear a sari,' said Renoir, so I got out a Benares silk sari and the rani haar or queen's necklace that Bikki—my husband Tikki's brother—had given me.

Taking jewellery to a foreign country was a nightmare in those days. This necklace was three strands of pearls with diamond and emerald clasps and a diamond and emerald pendant. There were diamond and emerald earrings to go with it and a bracelet, a river of green emeralds. It was all very expensive; besides the value of the stones, it was said to have belonged to some queen or the other. No doubt I had been told but I am no good at these details. So you had to get a description put on your passport and it had to be stamped when you were leaving the country and it had to be stamped again on your return or else you could be hanged by your toes for seven months and seven days for smuggling. Or something like that. (I know you're wondering why I'm telling you all this. Hang on.)

The play was magical as I had expected. As I rose to my feet to applaud, every woman's nightmare happened. The fat man who was sitting next to me stepped on my sari and the pleats came undone. He was appalled of course and started grabbing metres of the delicate silk and started pushing them in the general direction of my petticoat. Then he realised what he was doing and let it all go.

Renoir was grinning in the way men do when something happens that cannot happen to them. I sat down and did my pleats again and tried to pretend that nothing had happened.

But it was not over. On the way back, I had to return the

jewellery to the concierge's care. I thought it best that all of it go back into the hotel safe. When I was handing the necklace over to the concierge who went by the delectable name of M Gateau, the strings broke and suddenly pearls were rolling all over the lobby floor.

We were both on our hands and knees, when a flunky appeared with a message for the concierge. '*M Cartier est arrivé,*' he said.

And it was Cartier, jeweller to the world, standing there. From my position on the floor, I looked at him with interest. I did not have very far to look. He was Cartier and to put it politely, he was not very tall. But at that moment, he belied his stature. It was probably his company that had matched the pearls for the necklace and now he responded with superb French good manners. He sat me down in a corner, bustled everyone about and supervised the gathering of the pearls. Then he turned to me. 'With your permission Madame, I would like to take these back with me and restring them with double knots.'

He was M Cartier so I agreed. The next day, another young man in black and white livery arrived with a green and white box in which lay my necklace. There was no bill. It is a truth universally acknowledged that a Parisian concierge will know the ways of the world. I found M Gateau in the lobby.

'I have not been sent a bill, M Gateau,' I said. From the corner of my eye, I could see a man with beady eyes and pointed moustaches, peering intently at me from the questionable shelter of a potted palm. Nothing, I thought to myself, is going to ever hide you from people if you insist on waxing your moustache into the shape of the handlebars of a bicycle.

M Gateau smiled paternally. There is nothing a Parisian concierge enjoys as much as explaining the world to those who do not know it as well. 'I do not think there will be a charge for you.'

So I simply sent M Cartier a card with my thanks.

After I returned, stoked with poultry juice, I found that my regular table had been changed around.

'M Jacques,' I asked, 'why has my table been shifted?'

'Oh Madame,' he said, 'I really cannot tell you.'

My besetting sin has always been diffidence so I simply accepted that he could not tell me and settled down again at my table. Then I found myself looking straight at the beady-eyed man with the magnificent moustaches and a rather striking woman who was eyeing me with disfavour. He seemed to be sketching me.

I began to grow uncomfortable for there is nothing so ridiculous as trying to pretend one does not know that one is being sketched. If one holds still, it seems as if one is giving permission. If one doesn't, it seems rude.

The moustachioed man saw that I was not very happy. That didn't stop him from sketching but when he had finished, he came up to my table, twirled one of his ridiculous moustaches a little and said, 'You are going to be my next Madonna.'

That was when I recognised Salvador Dali. He invited me to a vernissage, a private showing, of his pen and ink sketches of Don Quixote. 'Come to Avenue Wagram at seven,' he said, 'and wear a sari.'

When I left the hotel, the Garde Républicaine was on horseback, blocking the traffic so that I could arrive safely. Since the Garde wear brass helmets from which horsetail-like plumes hang to go with their black and red uniforms, I was beginning to feel a little, how shall one say it, conspicuous? I tried to protest but I was told: 'We have our orders.'

Dali was waiting for me, beaming. He took me through the gallery, showing me each of the pictures. He explained his processes which seemed to me to be more about the dramaturgy of the artist than the works of art. He told me how he dipped sea urchins in squid ink and threw them at the easel to achieve certain effects. He insisted on inviting me to a private dinner party but I declined politely.

The next day Dali left for Spain. And somewhere in a mural in Spain, I became a holy mother too.

SIX

Three Rubber Bras and a Yellow Nose

The first sign of trouble was a shoe box. Inside it, I found three bras with rubber baggies tucked inside them. They were equipped with little nozzles so that they could be blown up to the appropriate size.

Since I had never shot a Hindi film before, I wondered who blew them up and who decided the appropriate size. Perhaps the heroine herself blew them up and then came out of her dressing room.

'No, Madamji, in this film, you are a 38B cup, remember?' an assistant director might say to her perhaps.

'Oops,' she'd say and go back to the nozzle again, to deflate or inflate her measurements.

I couldn't see myself doing any such thing so I returned the shoe box and almost ended my career in Hindi films, before it had started. I don't think this would have worried me much.

I did have an intense relationship with cinema from the time I had gone with my father to see *The Fall of Stalingrad*. I must have been about five years old, but I found myself completely drawn into the story. At one point, when it seems that the mother and child who were fleeing from Nazi soldiers are about to be caught, I could not restrain myself. 'Watch out,' I squeaked in terror.

My father took me out of the theatre and gave me a short, sharp lecture on film-watching etiquette. Then we went back to the theatre and I watched the rest of the film with a hankie stuffed inside my mouth. It still gives me goose-bumps to think about that film.

But I did not see myself as an actress. I enjoyed cinema and loved it, but I enjoyed music and dance too and was even said to have some little skill there. One of my earlier encounters with films was an abstract film made by a young man, George Salomon. He was an alumnus of L'Ecole Internationale in Geneva. He got hold of my number and called. Perhaps he had seen me in one of the amateur plays that we performed in the school or at the ballets that the ballet teacher staged from time to time. He said he was making an experimental film and would like me to play a part in it. We worked on the script together although, as a thirteen-year-old, I was not sure whether I made any contribution or whether he was just being kind when he listened to what I had to say.

It was called '*Leela où la fille qui veut égaler les dieux*' or '*Leela or the girl who wanted to equal the gods*'. There was no script. All I had was a framework and I was supposed to improvise movement around the five ideas that would animate the five scenes of the film, all set to a montage of Stravinsky music. George asked me to design my own costumes and so I put together a white tulle skirt and a white apron with black musical notes pinned diagonally across it. We shot the film on the weekends in the antechamber to the Salomon dining room with as many lights as George could beg, borrow or steal.

I do not know whether the film still exists so I shall try and describe it as best as I can.

The first scene had empty frames hanging from the ceiling of the room around which I move.

The first frame was me looking at a landscape, at this point I am only an observer. In the second frame I begin to sense that someone is looking at me. This frightens me. In the third frame I decide not to be frightened. By the fourth frame I am in attack mode. I shall confront whatever it is. In the fifth frame it's a game of chess into which I am invited. I play against a masked man, a stocking over his face. I am defeated. He strangles me on the chessboard since I am now part of the frame, victim of my hubris. My world goes up in flames.

Thinking about it now, I can see the film was rather heavy on symbolism. The frames were supposed to symbolise innocence, the tabula rasa of the young. The film's trajectory was also traditional, moving along the lines of the doomed hero, condemned by a fatal flaw in his make-up. But Salomon did a good enough job to impress the jury at the Amateur Abstract Section of the Cannes Festival and he won the first prize there.

I did not do the film as a first step to a career. I acted in it out of joy, out of the desire to experiment with movement and out of the desire to know what it felt like to move in a film as opposed to performing for a live audience.

My film career began with three frames that remained on a roll of photographic film. Kamala Chakraborty, the widow of Ameya Chakraborty, had been shooting textiles or handicrafts as part of the work she did with Pupul Jaykar. Then she came to visit us at Sujan Singh Park and since she had three frames left, she used them to take pictures of me.

And those were the prints that were lying on the table when Hrishikesh Mukherjee went to visit her. He took one look at them, so she told me, and said, 'She is my Anuradha.'

Then he asked, 'Who is she?'

Kamala told him that I was married to Tikki Oberoi.

'Oh God, not another socialite,' he said.

Kamala roundly castigated him for making generalisations. Perhaps that was why he had to work on her a little before she would give him any further details. When she called me to prepare me, she told me she had tried to dissuade him, telling him that I was not really interested in Hindi films. That set him back a bit. For like all inhabitants of hermetic, self-involved worlds, the denizens of

Hindi cinema cannot believe that there can be others unmoved by its tinsel attractions.

'How do you know?' he asked.

'She turned down Raj Kapoor and he wanted to sign her for four films.'

That was true.

In 1955, when we returned to India from Europe, we lived in Bombay as the guests of Dr and Mrs Baliga. During our stay, the good doctor asked me if I would like to accompany them to a wedding. I agreed because he assured me there would be jalebis. (Hot jalebis without chemical dyes in them were one of my favourites.)

'Wear a sari,' I was told. Doctors can be quite autocratic. But then most men can, given half the chance. I got into an orange Benaresi silk sari with delicate zari on it and put my hair up in a bun and got into the car that whisked us off to Matunga. It was only when I got down from the car that I realised that it was a filmi wedding. I did my namastés to a series of portly gentlemen. Later, Mrs Baliga told me that I had smiled politely and walked past two generations of Hindi cinema aristocracy: Prithviraj Kapoor and Raj Kapoor were at the doors, welcoming guests to Shammi Kapoor's wedding. That was where Raj Kapoor saw me the first time. He later made enquiries with the Baligas and was told that I was in Delhi.

And so one morning, when I was having my hair washed at Roy and James in Connaught Place, a tremulous little man came up bearing a card. It said. 'To a peeping face in a moving car. Would you and your father care to join me at the Imperial Hotel to discuss a project?' It was signed, Raj Kapoor.

I showed the card to my father when he got back from UNESCO. He knew even less about Hindi cinema than I did. But he did recognise the name Kapoor. 'I know one Kapoor. His name is Prithviraj Kapoor and he's a Member of Parliament.' Perhaps that was why my father and I agreed to go, because he knew a Kapoor but did not know how common Kapoor is as a surname in India.

Raj Kapoor turned out to be all perfume-scented (Worth's Je Reviens) politesse. He wanted to make Mulk Raj Anand's story, *The Goddess and the Tractor*, into a film. He had already spoken to Mulk who, as one of Daddy's oldest friends from their days in London as Fabian Socialists, was ecstatic. His prophecy seemed to have come true.

'I would like to prepare for the part by living in a village for a month or two,' I said to Raj Kapoor, who looked a little green. 'It will be hot . . . and there will be mosquitoes,' he murmured. But I did not think I could sit in a Delhi house and turn into a villager overnight. So I insisted as politely as I could. Kapoor looked at Daddy for help. Surely Dr Naidu could not wish his daughter to live in a village . . .

Surely Dr Naidu could. 'I do not see how a couple of weeks in a village could help Leela turn into a tractor or a goddess,' he said poker-faced, 'But we should let her try.'

'Right then,' sighed Raj Kapoor and we went away.

A few days thereafter, I went to Agra with some friends of the family. I had not seen the Taj Mahal and I wanted to. The friends did not turn out to be convivial companions. Their first response to that great illusion of immortal love, that perfectly proportioned dream in white marble, was to try and work out how much it would cost if it were to be built now. I was young enough to be sickened by this commercialism—perhaps I would still be but I think I might understand it a little better—so I wandered away from the group.

Outside the Taj Mahal there was an old man with a tonga who was feeding his horse and drinking some water. He offered me some of his water chestnuts, in a gesture that was so courteous, so simple and so full of old world charm, that to refuse would have been impolite. I paid for it, of course, with a bout of jaundice so severe that I was in bed for six months.

It was only after I recovered that I went to RK Studios. I had been warned by Janki Ganju of the Information and Broadcasting Ministry. He said, 'Raj Kapoor is a fine director but he has a regrettable tendency to fall in love with his leading ladies.'

Evidence of this regrettable tendency was present at RK Studios. Nargis supervised the entire shoot, producing clothes from the wardrobe for me to try on. Radhu Karmarkar prowled around, taking random shots. Some of the outfits I thought were a little slinky for a goddess (or a tractor!) but I did as I was told.

Finally, as I got into a black satin pantsuit, I could not stop myself. 'Why am I wearing this if I'm being screen-tested as a villager?' I asked.

That was when Raj Kapoor told me that he wanted me to do four films with him. I was supposed to sign a contract and I would be the next RK discovery. I said that I would think about it and I did think about it. At that time, I was set on going to Oxford. So I wrote a nice note to Raj Kapoor, turning him down.

Mrs Chakraborty told Hrishikesh Mukherjee all this but he persisted and came to Delhi with a script. It was in Devanagari, assuming perhaps that this would put me off reading it. But I had studied Devanagari and am comfortable in it. (In fact, I prefer my scripts to be in Devanagari if it is a Hindi film. It just seems to make more sense that way.) It was incomplete but I liked what I read and I knew the story of the film.

Today, almost every film is available in some format. All you need is the equipment and you can sit down to a video compact disc of a Satyajit Ray or a digital video disc of a John Ford. But in the 1950s, it was not so easy to see a director's work. However, a friend pointed out that *Musafir*, one of Hrishikesh Mukherjee's earlier films, was showing somewhere and I went off to see it. I did not think it an exceptional film but I did like the restraint. The film was about a guest house to which a series of people come and I remember thinking, 'Well, his heart is in the right place.'

Besides, Hrishida didn't just ask me; he practically asked my parents as well. Since he had studied mathematics, he got along well with Daddy.

Before I signed the film, my father announced that he wanted to talk to me. 'I have heard,' he said, 'that there is something called black money as opposed to white money. I trust that you will take your money in cheques and that you will pay your taxes. This is a poor country, you know.' I was a little surprised and a little hurt that he should think he would have to tell me that. But I was to fight many a battle with producers who approached me about the mode of payment.

'Madamji,' one of them expostulated, 'it is more expensive for us to pay you by cheque.'

'But Madamji,' said another, 'you will end up paying forty-six per cent tax.'

'Then I shall pay it,' I said.

I did not talk to Daddy for a fortnight after his warning. I don't think he noticed. Anyway, the upshot was that I signed *Anuradha* and found myself with a shoe box. I sent it back of course and refused to wear three satin petticoats. Mohan Studios had no air conditioning and three layers of satin? 'Madam, I am very sorry to do this to you,' said Mr Lulla, the producer, 'but the audience will think you have tuberculosis.' I did not think they would and I told him so in no uncertain terms.

Then came a struggle over the make-up. 'Why is the bridge of my nose yellow and my nostrils blue?' I asked.

'Your nose is too thin. This will make it look better,' I was told.

'I quite like my nose,' I said.

Then they wanted to extend my eyes with kaajal. It was a fashion called 'teer maaro teer' then and it was an attempt to emulate the Bani Thani painting of Kishangarh. I wiped it off. Next came a tray with two caterpillars. 'False eyelashes? On a country doctor's wife?'

Anuradha is the simple story of a musician who falls in love with a dedicated country doctor. She follows him to the village where he works, giving up her music and her creativity. Then a friend of hers comes to the village and catalyses a crisis in her marriage. The false eyelashes would have been what she would never have worn even as a performer and certainly not as a housewife in the middle of rural India. But in an industry dominated by tradition and a disregard for realism, my objections must have seemed a little odd.

But once I had managed to avoid being painted to resemble a clown, being stuffed to resemble a potato, we began work.

~

Hrishida did not direct; he suggested. He offered a few comments and then he left me to it. Once he did ask, after a shot, 'Do you rehearse in front of a mirror?'

'Of course not,' I said indignantly and he left it at that. In his own quiet way, he did seem fond of me. He invented a nickname for me: 'mukhpuri'. I once asked him what it meant. 'Rotten face,' he said.

I tried to look amused. 'To ward off the evil eye,' he said. I could have wished for a more polite way of doing that but I got used to the name and even enjoyed it after a while.

I do not remember my first day of shooting perhaps because I did not suffer from stage fright. According to me, stage fright is about waffling. It happens when an actor will not stay in the moment. When you begin to worry about your past—I've messed it up before—or your future—I may look stupid doing this—you aren't in the moment. And either you are in the moment, in the skin of the character, in the world you have created for that character or you're out. Either you believe in the myth that you are helping to create or you do not. There are no halfway measures.

I also earned the reputation of being a communist. One might think that on a Bengali set this would not be a problem, but I have always found that people are much more comfortable with isms in the abstract. Once any principle is put into action, everyone gets a little uncomfortable.

On the sets of *Anuradha*, a spot boy fell from the gangplank high above us and fractured both his legs. The crew seemed willing to continue as if nothing much had happened. I was appalled at this and went on strike. I refused to shoot until the poor man was taken to the hospital. They bundled him off the sets but I wanted to see the case paper and I wanted an assurance from the producer that he would pay the medical bills before I would start again.

While we were shooting the dance sequences at the beginning, I was surrounded by a host of twinkly ladies who were described to me as 'extras', a word I thought insulting and offensive. If anyone or anything is extra, it should be removed. If however, the people or props are needed, they cannot be called extras. But they were treated as if they were expendable. For instance, I was horrified to discover that only I had been assigned a chair, that there was nowhere for them to sit. They were all in costumes and could not sit on the floor for fear of dirtying or tearing the costumes for which they would have to pay. So I refused to sit on my chair. Perhaps they were afraid I would collapse so an assistant director was assigned to follow me around bleating, 'Please Madam, sit down Madam.' I told him that I would sit down only when everyone else could sit down.

'But that is difficult, Madam,' he protested.

'If you can get one chair, you can get thirty.'

He tried another tack. 'They are used to standing, Madam.'

'I see no reason why they can't get used to sitting down too,' I said and finally, after much grumbling, they arranged the chairs.

One of the major problems at the studios was the toilet. It was nothing short of a tragedy, so I asked one of the other dancers where they went. She pointed to the back of the studio where there were a huge number of stucco boards lying around.

'Go behind one of them,' she said, 'but be careful of the snakes.' If that was the only way to go, I decided I was going to hold on till I got home.

I think it would be unwise of me to comment on Balraj Sahni as an actor. He was obviously extremely good at his work. I loved him in *Do Bigha Zameen* (and later in *Garam Hawa*) which made me cry and cry. But he also did seem to lend his gravitas to many films that did not seem worthy settings for his talent.

Once I asked him why and he said: 'Leela, it's like running a race. You see the end, and want to reach it, and till you are overtaken by the quagmire, you keep thinking the end is still in sight.'

Sahni was a perfect gentleman. But like many other perfect gentlemen, he was not above trying his luck. One day he dropped me home from the studios.

'I think of you all the time,' he said.

'That's kind of you,' I said.

'You are in my head,' he said.

'And how is your dear wife?' I asked. I have found that this question generally manages to quench the libido of the perfect gentleman. It returns him to his suave self. But rejection also brings out a little imp.

Anuradha ends with me sweeping the floor, tears in my eyes. Balraj Sahni had other ideas. 'Perhaps,' he suggested to Hrishida, 'She should say something like, "Get me a kilo of tomatoes from the market."' I knew where he was going with that one. Saying something like that would mean a reaction shot. It would shift the focus from Anuradha's sacrifice to the doctor's response. Luckily, Hrishida saw it too and told him he would think about it. I never had to ask for tomatoes and was grateful that I didn't have to fight that one. Perhaps it was something to do with the fact that Hrishida was a mathematician. That showed in his cutting of the shots, which was precise and economical. It also showed in the logic in the exposition of his films. If the film was called *Anuradha* and the internal struggle was Anuradha's against her circumstances, it seemed odd that it should end on a kilo of tomatoes and a reaction shot from the circumstances!

SEVEN

'Who Am I Playing, Leela?'

I suppose word had spread that I was the kind of actress who wanted a script before she would sign on the dotted line. Of course, that was only metaphoric use because there were no proper contracts in those days, just a letter signed by the producer. I would be surprised if things are very different these days. So when R.K. Nayyar approached me, he told me that the film was based on William Saroyan's *Laughing Matter*. But it soon turned out that they'd decided that the book was about jealousy and the film would also be about jealousy. I would not have been able to find that out earlier because there was no script. But by then, if someone told me that they had a story idea beyond 'it is a love story, Madam, set in Kashmir' or 'it is a love story, Madam, with Shashi Kapoor', I considered myself lucky and so I agreed to do *Yeh Raste Hain Pyar Ke*.

I told Nayyar that I would not pop up from behind a bush and take a spin in a spinney of trees.

'Look, Leela,' he replied, 'if I told you to run around trees, you would do it tongue-in-cheek and it would show. That would ruin it.'

'Quite right,' I said and we got on fine after that. I was getting ready to play another wife when I got an urgent call. *Anuradha* had been sent to the Berlin Film Festival. Satyajit Ray met Hrishikesh Mukherjee there and asked him, 'Where is she?'

Mukherjee was a little nonplussed. 'Who?'

'Your Anuradha. Where is Leela?'

And so I was given a day's notice to fly to Berlin. I had a great time there, watching films and talking to all the interesting people who came to these festivals. Many of them were technicians and passionate about cinema in a way that few stars can be.

Hrishida then decided that it would be great fun for all of us to go to Paris. We were all short of cash but we went, Hrishikesh Mukherjee, Sunil Dutt, Nargis and I. It was a pleasure for me to be back in the city that I had walked through as a child, led by my father's friend, the architect. It was a pleasure simply to sit on a bench and watch lovers come and go and fight and make up near the Champs Elysées. But the men with me wanted a little bit of the high life so we went for a single meal to the George V, a very plush hotel. I had warned them that it would be expensive and ordered myself a frugal salad. Hrishida was busy running his finger down the right side of the menu and finally arrived at what he wanted to order. It was, as far as he could make out, the cheapest thing on the menu.

'This,' he said, pointing it out to the waiter.

The waiter inclined his snooty tête in the direction of the menu. Then a look of bewilderment began to spread over his face like a sauce over a pudding. He turned to me.

'*Seulement les curedents de porc-épic?*'

Hrishida had ordered porcupine quills, which were sold as elegant toothpicks.

We went to Versailles and I strolled in the gardens as the men wandered around the palace. When they had had enough, and were ready for lunch, I did what I have always done. Ask one of the people in the town where they would eat. I was directed this time to a small restaurant where we had a lunch of wild hare in mustard sauce, a house red and a salad. I did not eat the hare—I had had a rabbit as a pet—but the sauce was superb. The husband and wife team who ran the restaurant did all the work. She did the cooking and he maintained a kitchen garden and had a permit to shoot game. There was an apricot tart to follow, which was perfect. It was one of the best meals I had ever eaten.

Sunil Dutt asked if I could go to Spain and scout locations for *Yeh Raste Hain Pyar Ke*. I knew that my ticket could be extended but I was not sure that I had a visa that would work in Spain. I asked the French authorities and they assured me that a French visa was good for the whole of Europe. This was, of course, long before that agreement was signed in Schengen, Luxembourg, the one that made a single visa sufficient for fifteen European countries.

And so I flew to Madrid. At the airport I was horrified to discover that the French were wrong. The Spanish were outraged that the French should think their visa would suffice. They wanted a Spanish visa and they were going to deport me. I must have looked stricken at the thought and so the immigration officials decided to redirect their rage at the French officials who had misled me. Finally, one of them said he would give me one day to get a visa or else he would be forced to deport me.

I asked him for some advice. Where could I stay? Who would I have to meet? Soon the man was beaming in an avuncular fashion. He recommended a hotel that was walking distance from the office to which I would have to go and advised me to present myself at nine o'clock the following morning. After an uneasy night, I rose and was at the office on the stroke of nine. No one else was. I kept asking various people, but they were mainly the cleaning staff and seemed surprised that anyone should think that a Spanish government office would be functional at that hour. It was finally eleven thirty when the officer arrived and he had many pressing matters to deal with before he could attend to me. The most urgent of these seemed to be that his shoes had not been polished. 'Come tomorrow,' he said surveying his footwear with horror.

'At eleven?' I asked.

He looked up, startled. 'Madam, if you come at eleven, when will I get my shoes polished?'

Obviously, this was a man with his priorities straight. But after two days of suspense I finally got my visa for a three-month stay.

But another problem reared its head. I was on very short rations, since my foreign exchange was limited and my money was going to run out. Besides, I was still at the hotel, which was in front of the palace grounds. Like all hotels that are located in prime positions, it was expensive but its clientele didn't care much. They were all businessmen on expense accounts. As I walked around the Prado, I was wondering how one declared bankruptcy in another language and in a foreign city. Did they still have debtors' prisons in Spain?

Another couple of days and Sunil Dutt wired me the money. I could relax and go out for paella and some flamenco. There were flamenco shows at the hotel, of course, but I could tell that the performers were performers. They were not dancers. And so I asked an old waiter at the hotel where I could have real paella and watch some real flamenco. He gave me directions and I set out around eight o'clock and got there when they were still sweeping the floor. The cleaners told me to come back at ten or eleven or later perhaps. I must have looked somewhat disconcerted at the thought of wandering the streets for two and a half hours for one of them took pity on me and told me to sit down at the table. He brought me a rich bowl of paella and I ate as slowly as I could, spinning out the pleasure.

Then I walked to El Grotto for the flamenco. I cannot remember the name of the man who danced that night but he was an incredibly fine dancer. His sobriquet was 'El Duende' because it was said that he had fire inside him. Although he was past his youth, he brought all the fire and passion of the flamenco into his dancing. We did not see an old man with grey hair; in fact we did not see a man at all. We saw flamenco.

I walked Madrid, following cobbled pathways and alleys across the city. It was not difficult to find beautiful locations; everything offered itself as a possibility. Each morning I would have my breakfast in a little park near the hotel. There were small trolleys selling frittatas (crusty fried breads) and I would buy one piping hot and sit on the park bench and nibble it while the pigeons fluttered self-importantly around me and sparrows cocked their impertinent eyes at my breakfast.

A few days later, I returned to Mumbai and to R.K. Nayyar's set.

~

Agha Jaani Kashmiri was the dialogue writer on this one and he would bring the dialogue to us, every morning, flavoured with the biryani of the night before. There were two make-up men who seemed afflicted with the giggles. They carried a make-up trunk and when they opened it, I saw they had put their dirty shoes inside. I decided that I would do my own make-up from that moment on. They went off, unabashed and still in inexplicable giggles. Later, someone told me that they were addicted to bhang, a cannabis-based narcotic.

We were shooting in Filmalaya where before each shot, someone would have to shoo away the pigeons with a stick, thumping at the corrugated iron of the roof. But the cooing was not the only zoological disturbance. There was also a herd of goats. As soon as the red light of the 'No Entry' sign would go on, signifying that a shot was in progress, the owner would kick one of his goats and it would set up a terrific racket. I thought he was unusually cruel to his animals but discovered that there was a commercial motive to his behaviour. The assistant directors also discovered this and we could depend on the goats going unmolested as long as the goatherd was tipped on a regular basis. At first he only charged Rs 10 but as time went by he got a little greedier and soon his rate was Rs 150.

Speaking of shepherds, I am reminded of one of the last scenes that had to be shot for *The Householder*. This was the scene that Satyajit Ray would eventually put at the beginning of the film.

The character I was playing is very pregnant. I am on my way to Mehrauli, padded with towels, wrapped in a shawl. My mother and I were fairly sure that Merchant and Ivory would not have figured out a place for me to change, especially since this was to be an outdoor shot. So I dressed in my costume and bundled my 'pregnancy' under my petticoat. An old woman at the house in Mehrauli was very perturbed. 'Is she married?' she asked my mother. For some reason, she had mistaken me for the bride to be.

'I think so,' my mother said, much to the old lady's consternation.

'Chee chee chee,' she sighed. 'Nowadays, they get the baby first and then they marry.'

By then I had signed *Yeh Raste Hain Pyar Ke* and was expected back in Bombay. This meant that I had to finish the shot and rush back to Delhi airport. When it was over, I looked around for some place to change. We were in the middle of the Indo-Gangetic plain at its smooth unwrinkled best. Then my mother spotted a dry nullah.

'Hop into that,' she said. 'But watch out for the snakes.'

I suppose it was what I would have said in the situation but it was not very reassuring. The thought of a snake is bad enough; the thought of a snake when one is half-dressed is a bit trying. But luckily no reptiles showed up and I scrambled out dressed in my ordinary clothes. My mother was chuckling as I got into the car that was taking us to the airport.

'What happened?' I asked.

'Turn around,' she said, 'and wave.'

I didn't understand but I turned around and waved at a perplexed little shepherd boy who kept looking at the car and down into the nullah. Then it dawned on me that he had seen a pregnant woman leap into the nullah. A few seconds later a slim version of the same woman had emerged.

'But he was a brave boy with a big heart,' said my mother. 'He immediately jumped into the nullah. I think he wanted to save the baby he thought you had abandoned.'

It was a delight to work with Ashok Kumar. He was a great actor, but also one of a peculiar breed that could belong only to Hindi commercial cinema. Ashok Kumar would come on to the set and look around. He would greet everyone and seemed to be very much at home. Then he would come up to me with a wry smile and say, 'Leela, tell me, what is the name of the film?'

I would dutifully tell him the name of the film.

'And what is the name of my character?' I would tell him that too. 'And yours?'

He was generally on the second of the three shifts of his work day. Anyone who works on several films at a time is likely to get confused.

'Will you get them to write my character's name on the tripod of the camera?' he would ask and then vanish into his green room to get ready.

If I found that a little tiring the tenth time, I did not show it. There is no point losing your cool in a collaborative enterprise like cinema. Everyone has their idea of preparation and everyone has their idea of what constitutes a career. I had mine and Dada Moni had his.

However, he could be great fun too. In *Ummeed*, an unreleased film directed by Nitin Bose, I played his daughter. In one scene, he was supposed to be dying and I was supposed to approach his bed to take his blessings. The foot of the bed had been placed on a whole pile of bricks in order to raise it. This had something to do with the lighting.

Take one. I approach the bed, hopefully with the gait and bearing of a woman about to lose her beloved father. I lean over him and a maniacal cackle erupts from Dada Moni. Everyone, including me, jumped a foot. Dada Moni pulls out a laughing box, the kind of gadget young children enjoy and shows it to me. Obviously, the take was declared NG, or No Good. Many apologies and we begin again.

Take two. I approach the bed, etc. etc. It seems that my screen father was unwilling to die for another hysterical cackle erupted. The odd thing was that he managed to startle us all again. This seemed so gloriously funny to Dada that he began to laugh in earnest. He laughed and he laughed and suddenly the bricks were shaking and the bed was tottering and down they all went in a heap.

When everything was raised again, he died quite perfectly and with no retakes needed.

That was not always the case with other actors. In *Yeh Raste Hain Pyar Ke*, we had to shoot what was, on the face of it, a perfectly simple scene. Rehman was supposed to knock on the door. I open it. He has to say something like, 'I dropped by to give your children these chocolates.' Nothing more than that. No histrionics. No emotional complexities. No difficult blocking. No long speech. A single line. If anything, it was a scene that required me to get through a sequence of events. I am lying down. I hear the knock. I respond. I get up. I hush my disturbed children. I go to the door and open it, all in one shot.

And yet, it is part of the mystery of acting that this veteran of hundreds of films would simply dry up after he'd managed the 'good evening'. We used up thousands of feet of film as Rehman would start with his 'good evening' and then fall into an abyss of silence. By the twentieth take, as I rose once again, to hush my children and walk to the door, I was pleading with him in a little part of my head, 'Oh please Mr Rehman, please finish this stupid line and let us all get on with our lives.' But it went on and on and my face muscles ached as I kept trying to respond with the right mixture of surprise and suspicion that any woman might feel at a late night caller. Finally, someone suggested that Rehman be taken away and given a snifter. This was duly done and he came back, slightly flushed of face, and gave a perfect take.

But when we were shooting *Arzoo*, even the snifters had ceased to work. This was a film in which I preside over much of the action from behind glass and a garland. As the first wife of Rehman, I was preparing to die, as the script required me to, early in the film. Rehman muffed the first take but pretended he was doing it on purpose. I gulped back my tears, dried my face, and got back into position. He muffed the second take but said that he was practising. I asked him, 'Could you let me know when you are ready? Because I'm not using glycerine. I'm crying.'

He assured me that he was ready. So I mopped up again and affected some repairs to my make-up and got ready to die. The tears rolled, the cameras rolled but Rehman came to a standstill. It took him fourteen takes and left my eyelids feeling like sandpaper.

In the middle of the shooting of *Yeh Raste Hain Pyar Ke*, Commander Manekshaw Nanavati took his children and wife to a cinema hall and then went back to fetch his gun. He was going to see Prem Ahuja, who he felt had cuckolded him. He shot him dead and on 27 April 1959, he was accused of the murder. It was India's last trial by jury.

The distributors were delighted because there seemed to be a similarity between the two cases. They felt that the notoriety of the case—a Presidential pardon finally meant that the much decorated Commander Nanavati did not hang—would ensure the success of the film. I was appalled at this. I would never have agreed to do a film that sought to exploit someone else's tragedy. Besides, Nanavati's sister and I went to the same B.K.S. Iyengar yoga class at Campion School. I had to tell her that the film I was doing was in no way exploitative. But the buzz continued and the rumours spread so I called a press conference to deny the connection. It was the only press conference I have ever called and I hope the only one I will ever need to call.

I had been asked to block ninety-one days for the shoot. But after ninety-one days, I was still shooting. I did not ask about money; I have never been very good about commerce. All I wanted was a script or at least a synopsis, a directorial vision and a coherent character to play. When I am asked why I did so few films, I often feel like retorting that it was because I had very few requirements from a part in a film, but those requirements were too many for most Hindi film directors.

Sunil Dutt had taken over as the producer of the film. He was a thorough gentleman and when he heard that I was still working almost one hundred and fifty days later, he insisted I be paid. 'Her metre should be down and ticking,' he said.

R.K. Nayyar thought that the film should end with the husband and wife in love again. I was supposed to look at him (Sunil Dutt) with love in my eyes and then run into his arms. But the distributors up north were having none of it. She must die of a heart attack, they opined, or the audiences will not accept it. Like Sita, she has been stained. If Sita had to be banished, a mere mortal would definitely have to die.

I thought this was ridiculous. I had finished my final shots and I was not going to go back to work because some silly men thought that they should tell us what audiences would or would not accept. So my death scene was left out and I was 'cremated'. Thus two versions were shot—one for the cow belt and one for cosmopolitan audiences.

I also did a film called *Baaghi*. When the director Ram Dayal came to see me about the film, he offered me a thick green leather portfolio. I opened it, thinking that it would need a few days and found that it was a single page. The rest was filled with blank paper. Dayal had obviously assumed that I didn't actually mean to read the script.

'Who is the rebel?' I asked.

'You are, Madam. It is a costume drama.'

'And what costumes would we be wearing?'

'Rutu . . .' he began. 'Riru . . . Turi . . . Ritu . . .'

And then with the air of a man jumping off a linguistic cliff, 'Ruturania.'

Ah, so it was to be a Ruritanian film, set in the continent of European Royalist Fantasy.

'And you will design the costumes,' he said, pushing his luck. But I didn't mind and so put together Empire-style costumes.

Thus did it come to pass that I played a rebel princess and I had a maid who left little black patches of mascara on me, when she was supposed to weep in my arms. That maid was Mumtaz.

I don't remember much else about the film. It was a piece of nonsense and I am almost amnesiac about it. I don't think we understood each other, the Hindi film industry and I. They were always perturbed about something or the other that I was doing. In between shooting schedules, I would go riding or swimming.

'Look, you have gone so dark,' they would say.

'Yes, I have. Isn't it great?' I'd ask. This was the first time the colour of my skin had mattered to me. When I was young, my mother told me that I had once said apropos *de rien*, 'Daddy is café, Maman is milk and I am café au lait.' But the good producers could only see my tanned skin as unattractive.

'We will have to put pancake on you,' they insisted.

'Nothing of the kind. Show me in a garden and the viewers will understand that I've gone a little brown.' I thought a nice outdoors tan was healthy. I seemed to be in a minority of one as far as that opinion went.

EIGHT

A Man Possessed

The first time I met Ismail Merchant and James Ivory, they had an idea. They wanted to make a film based on an anthropologist in the deserts of Rajasthan.

'It will be set in a village,' said Ismail, bubbling with the enthusiasm that I soon discovered was his trademark. 'And it will have lots of camels and mosquitoes.'

I must say I doubted whether the idea would have immense appeal but I kept my reservations to myself. A few months passed and one evening, in the middle of compering a superb Romanian dance performance, I felt a tug on my sleeve. It was Ismail Merchant and he looked a little green about the gills. 'Please come, Leela,' he said.

On the stage, the Romanians were dancing. At my sleeve, a worried Ismail and behind him, James Ivory, in the darkness of the wings, a position he enjoyed. I told him I would meet them at the coffee shop of the Astoria after the performance.

'Can't you come now?' asked Ismail.

I couldn't. I was in the middle of a performance—I was doing a job but Ismail was always blinkered when it came to anything that concerned him. I did meet them later though and he poured out his woes while the Bostonian Baba sat quiet, his lips zipped. There was no money forthcoming for the anthropologist beleaguered by mosquitoes and surrounded by camels. Not even if Shashi Kapoor was in it, could I imagine.

I could actually.

We talked for a while and then I told him about a beautiful novel I had just read. It was *The Householder* by Ruth Prawer Jhabvala, who lived in Delhi. I had loved it for accuracy of detail and for the nuances of the relationship that was developing between two young Indians, caught between the modernity of the city and the memory of the village.

That evening at the Astoria's coffee shop, I told the pair to go off and read the book. The next thing I knew they were in Delhi talking to Ruth.

I once asked Ruth, later, when we were making the film, how she, a Jew married to a Parsi architect, caught the two young Hindu people so well. She said, 'I'm nearly blind, Leela. So I rely on my ears.'

'Your ears become our eyes,' I said. I was rather proud of that line but now thinking back, it seems a little inelegant. But she knew what I meant.

She would telephone me every evening to ask how the shooting had gone. I soon discovered that she was actually quite diffident about the dialogue she had written.

I remember telling her, but only because she asked me, 'Your dialogues have to breathe. Your sentence constructions must follow breath.' She took the advice to heart but she would still call to find out if the dialogue was sounding all right. I would do my best to reassure her until it occurred to me that it might help if I actually did detail any minor changes that we had made as we spoke. But Ruth's dialogue was very rarely stilted so those were a few spontaneous inversions.

Shashi Kapoor and his family and I were ensconced in the Swiss Hotel in Delhi. Jennifer was with him and his two sons. Kunal insisted on calling me Leelabai, the name of their ayah. Jennifer was horrified but I didn't mind, especially since he was quite a lovely child. One morning, we were sitting on the veranda, when the make-up man arrived to do me up. My skin is thin and reflects the light so I don't need much. My face and neck were covered in flesh-toned pan-stick, and a napkin was around my neck and shoulders. The make-up man was holding up a mirror in front of me. Kunal jumped to what he thought was the obvious conclusion: 'Leelabai is having a shave.'

Shashi was charming and he knew it too. Jennifer once said to him in my hearing, 'Why don't you act?'

'I am acting, Jennifer,' he protested

'No, you were not,' she said dryly. 'You were fluttering your lashes.'

And when shooting commenced in an old barsati that Ismail had found, right next to the Moti Masjid so that the mosque's dome became part of the mise en scène, Shashi would wave to the crowds that gathered on neighbouring terraces, enjoying the adulation. This was a little disconcerting since it only encouraged more people to come up and obstruct the skyline but he was too good-tempered—and good-looking—a man for one to resent it too long.

The family who owned the house and lived beneath did not interfere with the shooting. They did not even charge Ismail any money, something I think he was unduly proud of. In fact, they helped us in their own way. I had no idea how to make chappatis for instance and the matriarch coached me until I got them right, slapping the dough between my hands, and slowly flattening it.

As strict vegetarians, they weren't very happy when their old copper thalis were being filled with steaming mutton biryani (with a hovering *garni* of flies) for the crew's lunch. This was in the time before Ismail discovered his talent as a chef and before he could get people to act in return for his curry feasts. I was eating my rabbit food—salad and some bread and hard cheese—so it didn't bother me. James was already surrounded by a coterie of society ladies who kept him in asparagus and artichokes.

But I did feel that we were taking advantage of their generosity and so I spoke to Ismail about it. He made sure that the caterers brought their own utensils. The family would no doubt have preferred it if we had been vegetarian, but they simply averted their eyes and gave thanks that it was not their dishes being despoiled.

Ismail was obsessed with the film. He couldn't believe that it could not be completed in one long continuous shot. One day, he walked on to the set and found that we were all sitting around.

'Why are you wasting my money?' he angrily asked the cinematographer. 'Get on with it.' He was speaking to Subroto Mitra, the man who had shot all of Satyajit Ray's films, on loan to Merchant and Ivory and I think, the source of much of the film's beauty. Mitra was not unduly disturbed by Ismail's histrionics. 'I cannot shoot when there are clouds in the sky,' he said.

Ismail stared up at the clouds, fiercely. It seemed that he was trying, by force of will alone, to disperse them. Then he gave up and vanished on some errand, probably to do with the finance—or the lack of it—of the film. He was a very tense man, a tension that kept him at it, all day long.

Subroto and I got on well. He wasn't very happy on the set. He had worked with an auteur who knew exactly what he wanted. Ray would draw his frame, and even put in the lights, and say where he expected them to come from, what he wanted them to illuminate. James couldn't draw and he didn't seem to want to think his shots out either.

'He is always asking me where I should put Leela, where I should put Shashi,' said Subrotoda.

I tried to calm him down. I tried to ignore the heat on the terrace—remember this was Delhi in April as I walked across it barefoot. I tried to ignore the blisters that developed on my feet.

But I didn't know what to make of Merchant–Ivory when a child died in the house in which we were shooting. The family had not disrupted shooting, not even told us that one of their little ones was ill. When I came into the house and saw her lying on a charpoy, covered in white, I went to sit with the grieving ladies.

We did not talk. I held their hands. One of the men asked me if I could help organise a hearse. I got up to do so when an imperious voice called from above.

'Leela, what are you doing down there? Come up here.'

It was Ismail.

That was what dedication meant to him, blinkers that could even blot out human tragedy around him. He knew what he wanted and he would let nothing stand in his way.

In direct contrast was James whose indecision was almost chronic. To make matters worse, we were making a bilingual film, in English and in Hindi. I could not understand why we were making the film in Hindi. The power of *The Householder* lies in the way the writing looks in at a young family, looks in at it from a considerable if compassionate distance. The Hindi version was never going to achieve that, not just because Ruth wasn't writing it but also because language matters deeply in these things. I think I was proved right when I went to the world premiere at the Rockefeller Center, New York. When I came out, a group of very elegant elderly American women came up to me and one of them said, speaking for all of them, 'As Indu, you opened a window onto India for us.'

James dithered about whether we should speak in singing English of the kind that foreigners assume Indians speak, or say our lines straight. But Shashi and I decided that we weren't going to put on any accents or play to expectations. We would speak as we normally spoke.

I wasn't quite sure whether either James or Ismail knew how things happen on a set. There is a scene in which both Indu and her husband are invited to a tea party at the house of the college principal. Indu has developed a sweet tooth during her pregnancy and her husband is worried that she will shame him by putting her snout into the trough. But when the principal, a pompous buffoon (played by Romesh Thapar), encourages one of the ladies to sing, Indu sneaks in some Mysore pak. Just as the coy lady sitting next to Indu begins singing, Indu bites into it. The crumbly sweet does what it does best; it crumbles and leaps into the lap of the chanteuse. It was not something I had planned.

'Do it again for the Hindi version,' said Ismail.

'Sheer fluke,' I said.

'Stage it then,' he said.

'I can't,' I said.

I wasn't being difficult. I couldn't stage it because I never staged anything. Don't ask me what I'm doing with my hands or my feet or my face. I believe that if you know what one part of your body is doing, or you're planning what your eyebrows are going to do, you're not acting, you're modelling. The body is a tool but it is a tool that demands complete use. To use only a bit of it, or to focus on the bit that is visible in the camera frame, is to misuse the tool.

One day, when we were watching the rushes, Subrotoda began to rumble as he watched a particular shot. It was the sequence in which Indu is on a hunger strike, sitting cross-legged on the bed.

'Good work with the toes,' he said.

Toes?

I looked at the shot again. I was supposed to be sitting there immobile as Prem, played by Shashi, tries to get me to eat. That was when I noticed that my big toe was twitching, beating time, beating out the anger Indu feels in that scene.

I learnt all this by instinct. What Renoir gave me was a basic understanding of the way in which a text was only a framework and how each interpretation brought something new to that framework. What working with James Ivory did was to throw me back on to my own resources because he said almost nothing.

NINE

'She Has No Bad Angles'

I think too much has been made of my being listed by *Vogue* as one of the five most beautiful women in the world. My friends tell me that there has been some misguided attempt to quantify feminine beauty and that they have even tried to devise a unit to measure it. I believe it is called a Helen and each female face is measured in milli-Helens or in the number of ships that face might launch. One thousand milli-Helens make one Helen and so one thousand ships would go out to war. That sounds ridiculous because beauty is one of the most subjective of the abstractions and standards change. In Vatsyayana's time, it was a compliment to say of a woman that she walked like an elephant. Today, the same might be used as a putdown. Finally, it does boil down to the luck of the draw. This little strand of DNA brings you eyes of a certain colour; that one decides your hair; another, the shape of your jaw or the proportion of your collarbone to your neck. There's not much achievement in that.

But it did happen.

It was in New York after the premiere of *The Householder*. There I was, minding my own business, dressed in a natier-blue Chanel suit to appear on the Johnny Carson Show, and in my bag there were my Mughal earrings, when I was told that my agent was calling.

'Look, Leela,' said R.K. Nayyar, 'if I told you to run around trees, you would do it tongue-in-cheek and it would show. That would ruin it.' A tiny hint of that quality peeks out of this picture.

Leela at the age of eight: 'At one point, a photographer in Geneva asked Maman if he could photograph the two of us. He was excellent at these compositions of women wearing black sheets with only their hands and faces as contrasting areas of light.'

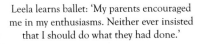

Leela learns ballet: 'My parents encouraged me in my enthusiasms. Neither ever insisted that I should do what they had done.'

Geneva, 8th January 1950

Darling daddy,

How are you? I hope you are not tired from the journey; we are getting on very well and I do all my best to obey Mummy and I am becoming independant but I am so sad that you are gone, the house seems empty but I take patience.

The weather is like spring

Letter from Leela to her father

but this afternoon it is misty it's a pity.

I am impatient that the school and the music lessons begin again from tomorrow. I am studying hard my piano it's fe a sorte of game to learn new pieces more difficult than the others, in waiting that the school starts I am reading Suffi books like "Jataka Tales" and pray with feeling.

I am very excited to go again and my beloved INDIA, it's quite funny to think that when I left Bombay I was only a little chum of 7. and that now I go on my 10th years and it's really impressive.

I have seen a beautiful film "The son of Lassie" it's a story of war in Norway when the germans occupied Norway and the strory of an English soldier Carryclaugh with his dog Laddie.

Longing to see you again your loving Lila with big kisses

Lila

PS. Mummy hugs you tenderly.

Leela with her father,
Dr Ramaiah Naidu

With her mother, Marthe
Mange, who had been
a journalist with *Le Petit
Democrat Populaire*

Leela in one of the gardens she loved.

Studio portrait

Leela in an uncharacteristic pose, very uncharacteristic

'Chopin was my first love. I loved his music and I wanted to learn to play the piano.'

Publicity stills

'I'm between two stools but I am not falling. I can understand the Europeans and I am at home in India. I can grow roots anywhere.'

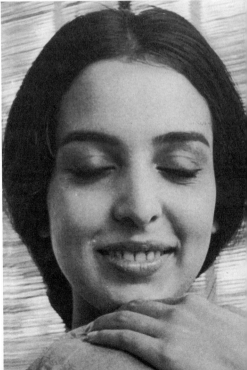

With Tikki and Bikki Oberoi.

With Tilak Raj (Tikki) Oberoi. Leela was warned against the hubris of trying to save someone.

Leela shortly after her wedding.

With Tilak Raj Oberoi and the twins: Maya and Priya. J. Krishnamurthi told Leela that she would always see her children as if from behind glass.

Shashi Kapoor and Leela worked together in *The Householder* and shared a special rapport.

If Raj Kapoor was unhappy that Leela turned down an RK contract for four films, he doesn't look it.

With Bollywood royalty: Raj Kapoor and Dilip Kumar flank the young woman

Leela Naidu and Sunil Dutt (second from left), a co-star she described as 'a limited actor and a perfect gentleman'.

The 'very British' Dom asked for Leela's hand in marriage. Here seen with (l to r), Marthe Naidu, the officiating priest, the bride, Dom Moraes and his mother Beryl.

With Imelda Marcos, who presented Leela with a signed copy of a book on Imelda by Imelda from the Ladybird imprint, better known for its fairy tales.

With Ferdinand Marcos. Dom was at work on *A Matter of People* and Leela was 'unpaid secretary making endless notes and translating his mumbling questions to puzzled people across the globe'.

No one can imagine *Trikaal* without the magisterial presence of Leela Naidu. It is odd to think that Shyam Benegal's first choice was Madhur Jaffrey.

For many years, Dom and Leela seemed to be the perfect couple.

Leela, shortly before she passed away.

Photograph by Chirodeep Chaudhuri.
Hair and make-up by Rayomand N. Sarkari.

It was indeed Marvin Minoff and he was in a hurry. 'Get to this address,' he said. 'As soon as the show is over, go there.'

'For what?'

He sputtered incoherently. 'It's starting to snow. If you can't get a taxi, just walk. Better still run. But get there.'

Then he hung up. I finished the interview and went out into the snow. It was falling steadily, not enough to turn the city white, not enough to be romantic, but enough to panic New Yorkers into taxis. So I walked eight blocks in my pumps until I got to the address. I read the name plate and felt a little shock of recognition. I had just walked all the way to Bert Stern's studio. For those who have forgotten, this was the man who had been granted the last photography session with Marilyn Monroe, six weeks before her death. Although all the 2,571 pictures had not then been released to the public, he was still riding high on that and here I was in a damp Chanel suit and snowflakes, panting and windblown.

His studio was this enormous hangar-like thing and he took one look at me and said, 'Oh my God, I can't shoot you in that suit, and you aren't wearing make-up.'

I had no idea what that meant. He had an awful tutti-frutti Kanjeevaram sari among his props.

'Where is the blouse?' I asked.

'Don't have one,' he said.

'So am I supposed to be an Indian widow, then?' I asked.

He arched an eyebrow at me.

'Only widows in India go around without blouses,' I said.

He roared with laughter and then looked at me again with the eye of a horse-dealer examining a filly.

'We can do without the blouse,' he said, 'because your collarbones are straight.'

My hair was draped in front of me, along the sari border. No make-up, just lipstick and a pencil line on my eyelids. I sat down on a seat that looked like a toadstool in the middle of the hangar, hung with klieg lights. His sixteen, I counted, his sixteen glorious ephebes danced about me, shooting Polaroids to capture my best angles before their master got down to work. That was when he shouted at them, 'Can't you see she has no wrong angles?'

Later I discovered how this had all fallen into place. Jules Stein, one of the owners of the Musical Corporation of America (MCA), had invited me to his Manhattan apartment for a party. I took up my position, found a vantage point from which I could watch without being watched. Then I settled down.

After a while, an elderly man came up to me. 'You remind me,' he said, 'of the young Greta Garbo.'

I was rather startled. For me, Garbo would always be the Nordic goddess standing at the prow of her ship in the last scene of *Queen Christina*. Her face is an endless enigma simply because the director had told her to hold it still and think of nothing at all. That Garbo and me?

'No, not in your appearance,' he said, 'but in the way you study the people in a room. She did not care much for parties but when she did go for one, it was only to watch people.'

As we talked, he told me that he was Garbo's 'major domo' and was looking after her. It was at this party that Consuela Crespi, the editor of *Vogue*, had seen me and set the whole thing in motion. In the end when the pictures were shot, it was decided that I would feature in the list of the five most beautiful women in the world. As they say in the Big Apple, that and fifty cents would have bought me a cup of coffee. Perhaps I didn't let my head get turned because at home I was never made to feel I was anything special because of the way I looked.

At one point, a photographer in Geneva asked Maman if he could photograph the two of us. He was excellent at these compositions of women wearing black sheets with only their hands and faces as contrasting areas of light. He was also very persuasive so Maman agreed. The next thing we knew, he had blown up the picture of me—I was twelve years old at the time—and had it made into a huge enlargement that he hung outside his studio on the lake.

But when people pointed and stared when I was walking with my father, he would brush it off. 'You must have a paper fish stuck on your back,' he said.

(In those days, children would sneak up to you around Easter and pin a paper fish to your back, as a prank. This was because the fish as Icthus was an ancient Greek symbol for Christ.)

And so I did not think too much about being considered one of the most beautiful women in the world. It was far more important to me that *Mademoiselle* magazine honoured me with a merit award for signal achievement in films. I was in the company of Susan Sontag who had been awarded for her writing, Barbra Streisand for her music and Valentina Tereshkova for her bravery in becoming the first woman to travel into space. That was a huge honour.

After both these events, some well-intentioned friends suggested that I should call press conferences. I refused to do any such thing. There seemed to be something unattractive about calling attention to oneself in such a manner.

~

I was ready to leave America when I got a call from my agents. Would I please go to Hollywood? Of course, I would, but once again: could I? After all, I was a young woman who was just starting out on her career, and Hollywood was a distant expensive place in the sun. But once again, my father's network of friends came to the rescue. B.K. Nehru was then India's ambassador to the United States of America and he and his wife were going to be in Hollywood at the time. They invited me to spend a few days with them at the Beverly Hills Wiltshire.

They had been invited to Pickfair, Mary Pickford's home and they took me along. At that time, two gossip columnists ruled Hollywood. One of them was Louella Parsons; the other was Hedda Hopper. Louella found out I was in Hollywood for a screen test and wanted to interview me.

'Where's your elephant and your mink?' she asked.

'Pink elephants? I don't have any. And I hate wearing fur,' I replied.

'I'll find you if I need you,' she said.

It sounded ominous.

At Pickford's sumptuous home, she found me. She said that she wanted to talk to me again. Pickford had a platinum blonde significant other who was sent to show me her wigs. I did not think I would enjoy this much but when we got there, the beautiful young man and I, the sheer excess took me by surprise. It was not just a rack of wigs, not even a cupboard full, but an entire room of the best wigs. Since these are always made of human hair, there was something odd about her collection, like a body parts spare room. The next time I would be in a room confronted with such excess was when Imelda Marcos took me to see her collection of shoes.

When I came back down, Parsons had left, and so I was spared any more facetious questions.

When the Nehrus left Hollywood, I moved into the Young Women's Christian Association hostel, which, in Hollywood, was a very safe place and designed as a hacienda with a terracotta-tiled roof. It was spotlessly clean and no one could call you up or harass you because they would have to get past the telephone operator. The head of the local branch of the YWCA who took me there was weeping, tears running down her cheeks from under her dark glasses. I was a bit puzzled by this and even began to feel a bit sorry for her when she said in a matter-of-fact voice, 'It's just the smog. It makes my eyes water.'

The first American film I did was called *A Face in the Sun*, a television film for Universal Studios. It was directed by the Canadian director Harvey Hart. It began so easily—Hart did not even want me to do an audition because he had seen *The Householder*—that I should have been suspicious. After I had signed on the dotted line, we went through an impressive rehearsal. Not a single detail was left out. All of us had our files with shot break-ups and schedules. Late on a Friday, someone thought to check my status as an actor. That was when my agency told them, oh dear, someone musta slipped urp because gee whiz we didn't get her a work permit.

Shooting was supposed to commence the following Monday. The set was ready. All the technicians had gathered. It wasn't one of those gigantic Hollywood films in which millions of dollars would be wasted if the shooting were postponed for even a day, but it was still a lot of people who would be out of work. And it was Friday evening and the whole of America was slamming its desk drawers, locking its cupboards and preparing for the weekend.

Oddly, I felt responsible. So once again, I got on to the phone to B.K. Nehru. He called the governor of California. The governor of California, who must have been slightly bemused by this request from the Ambassador of India, interceded with whoever it is who issues these permits. And when the phone rang and I was asked to send someone to pick up the temporary work permit, latest by five in the evening, that would allow me to act in Hollywood, there was a spontaneous cheer from the entire unit.

A Face in the Sun was quite a simple story. My character, Anna, gets off a train at a small station at a university town. And there, English literature professor, Professor Joseph Howe (Jason Evers), sees her and falls in love with her. Anna is something of a woman of mystery. She is en route from somewhere and the train has set her down for a day. In the end, she leaves again in a cloud of steam.

For this one, as for Anna's arrival at the station, we had to shoot a scene with a steam engine. And so we went to the Universal set where an old and beautiful train with a steam engine waited to produce the billowing steam into which various faces had vanished over decades.

After I had finished the shot, I heard the sound of someone clapping. I turned around and suddenly, there was a fat man with a face like a bull-dog.

'Beautiful,' he sighed.

Even then, everyone knew that Alfred Hitchcock had a predilection for blonde women so I looked around for a Nordic goddess.

Harvey Hart came up. 'Meet my assistant, Alfred Hitchcock.'

Hitchcock vouchsafed us a lugubrious smile. Then he pointed to the engine. 'She is beautiful, isn't she?'

The steam engine train was his favourite, he explained as he ran a plump and well-cared-for hand over its gleaming black flanks. Behind that impeccable boiled shirt, there beat the heart of a little boy.

Harvey Hart was dying to meet Renoir. We visited him in his house in Los Angeles, a reproduction of a Provençal farmhouse. There was a bronze bust of the boy Renoir by his father, Auguste—and this time it was a real Renoir.

Renoir was delighted to see me and so was Dido. He said he had seen two of my films at the University of California and Los Angeles. I figured out that those might be *Anuradha* and *The Householder*.

Over a simple lunch, he suddenly asked, 'Ça va? Ton A à Z?' (How is it going? Your A to Z?)

It still goes on.

TEN

Leela Naidu, Producer

I was at the Beirut Film Festival to which the Indian government had sent me on the grounds that 'everyone there spoke French', when my agent, who was David Niven's son, rang me from Rome with the news that David Lean was looking for me. I was put on to the next airplane to Rome after the festival. At the MCA office in Rome, I was told that Lean was in Madrid, where he was casting for a new film. Off I went, another aeroplane, another European capital. As I went through the doors of a beautiful boutique hotel in Madrid, I saw Lean himself, posting an envelope in the letter box that stood in the lobby.

I greeted him and was startled to see that he looked aghast. I had met him with Sam Spiegel in India and I thought we had had an interesting conversation . . .

'You saw me posting that letter? It was to Geraldine Chaplin. She was my second choice for the role.'

That was for the role of Tonya in *Dr Zhivago*.

Do I regret it? To say that I don't would be silly. To say that I do would be pointless. I shall simply say that my consolation prize was a lovely lunch with David Lean and a visit to the Prado.

Was that enough? When you are young and the sun is shining on the plain in Spain, and you have just spent a pleasant hour or two examining, among other masterpieces, Hieronymus Bosch's *The*

Table of the Seven Deadly Sins and Velázquez's *Dwarf Sitting on the Floor* and Goya's *Saturno* who looks horrified at his own savagery . . . well, it suffices.

My agents were also disappointed and I was called to London. I went to work on an ITV film for their *Man of the World* series. I played a doctor, a kind of *médécin sans frontières*, fighting the plague in India while an enemy advances.

One day, and this was in 1962, the art director spread out a map and asked me to take a look at it. He asked me where I thought the Chinese would attack India, were they to attack.

I had no idea why they were asking. I was supposed to be Leela Naidu, actor, not Leela Naidu, political expert or even Leela Naidu, war correspondent. But I looked at the map and saw the name Bomdila. I liked its bounce and its ring so I suggested that we use the name. Later, when the Chinese attacked in 1962 it was at Bomdila. ITV was delighted that their film had proved prophetic.

Around this time, I took stock. There seemed to be few films around that I wanted to do. I thought it might make sense to make films instead of working in films I felt nothing about.

～

The first film I ever produced started when I was put under house arrest. I was not a guest of the Indian government but had been interned by Kamalini Khatau. She had studied psychoanalysis with Anna Freud and had set up the BM Institute of Child Development in Ahmedabad. As a concerned parent and as a human being interested in children, I wanted to make a serious study of child psychology so I was a frequent visitor. I would borrow books from their library and one weekend when I visited, Mrs Khatau told me that she wanted a film to be made about her school, the Sharada Institute within the BM campus.

I immediately loved the idea. 'Oh Kamalini, that would be lovely. There is something about children with special needs that . . .'

'I am so glad you like the idea. I want you to make the film.'
'Me?' I squeaked.
'Yes, you will produce the film.'
'And who is going to write the script?'

She gave me a speaking look and I began to get the idea. That was when she told me her master plan.

'I am going to lock you up in my villa in Shahi Baug. You will have lots of paper and pens and pencils. Someone will come with your meals. But you will only come out when you have finished the script.'

I know this sounds difficult to believe but I went docilely into the house and settled down to write. I know I was an adult and didn't have to listen. I could have laughed politely, taken my books and gone back to Bombay. But I went into the house, sat down at the table and began to think. I must have wanted to do it.

It was difficult to sort out all that I knew about the children at the Sharada Institute. There was Manu, mentally retarded as the phrase went in those days, but also spastic. He was making slow progress at the school but his father, a sweet-maker in the old city, wasn't very bothered about that. It was clear that he was proud of his son. He didn't just love Manu in the way that one might love a 'difficult' or a 'problem' child. He brought his son to school every day and would often bring stacks of piping hot jalebis for all the other children. There was a south Indian girl whose father was in the army. She was also developmentally challenged, but she could speak smatterings of five different languages, including a little English. There was little Pappoo, infra-occlusive (which meant that her lower jaw stuck out), blind in one eye and whose mental age would never rise very far beyond one. And yet when the tabalchi came and the music began, Pappoo's plump body would begin to respond and a beatific smile would pass over her face.

If this film had to avoid the Scylla of condescension and the Charybdis of sentiment, it must look at these children and tell their stories. Keeping that in mind, I started to write.

When I came out of the house, two days later, Mrs Khatau read the script and declared that she liked it. She said that she would get some other psychiatrists to look at it, just in case there were any flaws in my understanding of the science of child development. When the doctors had approved the script, I ventured to ask Mrs Khatau what kind of budget she envisaged.

'Whatever you can get,' she said. I goggled at her a bit. I had expected that the Institute would be paying but clearly I had expected wrong. Mrs Khatau thought that the government should pay and so I worked out a budget—which is always a painful exercise for me—and put together a proposal for the film. Mrs Khatau then bulldozed her way through the bureaucracy and we were soon in the bowels of the Ministry of Information and Broadcasting or whatever its equivalent was called in the government of Gujarat.

The gentleman behind the desk liked the script. He liked the idea. But he had no money. Mrs Khatau fixed him with a look. Well, he had *some* money. But who was the director?

'Kumar Shahani,' I said.

'Never heard of him,' said the bureaucrat.

'That's because it will be his first film,' I said.

'But then why are you paying him so much?' asked the bureaucrat.

'Because he is a sensitive person, a gold medallist from the Film and Television Institute of India and he is the right person to direct this film,' I explained.

'Give him less,' said the bureaucrat.

At this point I could have thrown the proposal at his head and marched out but the thought that we might be able to do some good with this film kept me in my chair. We went through the same process for K.K. Mahajan, who I wanted as the photographer.

Finally and grudgingly, the government agreed to give us some money. I would have to raise the rest and it would be reimbursed to me when the film was done. (Need I say that I am still waiting for the money?) And so I simply took some mortgages on the few securities I had in my name, including some life insurance policies, pawned my jewellery and put my crew together. *A Certain Childhood* was directed by Kumar Shahani and photographed by K.K. Mahajan. The music was by Vanraj Bhatia, who was often a visitor at Sargent House where he would play the piano with fingers made a little oily by my mother's French fries. The Khataus gave us free accommodation.

One day Kamalini told me that she had shown the script of my film to Erik Erikson, the world-famous German developmental psychologist and psychoanalyst who was her guest in Ahmedabad.

'He wants to meet you,' she said.

I thought he would have something to say about my script, but he only asked me why I was borrowing so many books on child psychology and development.

'Because I would like to train as a child psychologist,' I said.

He told me that it would take many years. He explained that if I had found nothing of worth to do in front of the camera, I should think about working on the other side of it. And he gave me a copy of his *Young Man Luther: A Study in Psychoanalysis and History*.

'The young Luther,' he said gently, 'was filled with hubris. As a young man, he thought he could change the world, he could change religion.'

Kamalini must have told him something about my past, I thought. I believe he was trying to explain that the hubris of youth was a condition that arose from the feeling that anything was possible, that there was no sense of limitations, that there was no intimations of mortality. To try and change someone else was to believe that one could do anything one wanted to do, as long as one wanted it enough. The only person one can change is oneself.

That is what I believed his message to be.

It was an important moment in my life, a significant meeting. It turned me in a certain direction and when we began shooting, it was with a new sense of where I wanted to go.

One of my key shots was the children sitting on the bare floor of the auditorium and working with paints. Pappoo was chosen for this shot and her one eye lit up at the thought of painting. Mahajan wanted a fairly tight frame so he set up his tripod quite close to her. Pappoo began to paint, squinting as she went about industriously filling the paper with colour, dribbling a little as she daubed happily, cooing to herself as she let her paints spill out of the paper and following them where they led her. This took her, of course, to the wooden legs of the stand, the tripod, and soon she was painting all over the lens. It was a lovely shot, even if we had to cut the last few seconds of it.

Many doctors wrote to me after that, saying that the film had managed to capture some of the special quality of those who are developmentally challenged. It was the first film of its kind in India and much of its success came from the fact that the children were comfortable while they were being filmed and they smiled at the camera, sudden sunburst smiles that made one aware that there was a purity in their responses. You have to only watch a child with special needs confronted with jalebis, or listening to a tabla and you see pure unalloyed happiness. I thought that they were doing a great job and kept the commentary to a minimum, as if the words were captions to pictures in an album.

It was a bit of a letdown after that to make commercials, but they presented their own challenge. The film on Terene was particularly trying. How was one to represent what this synthetic fabric was, how it was made, what it could be used for, how it was very fashionable and how you could be a beautiful person wearing it, all in one minute? And then there was the maker of Armour Shirts who was very keen that we show all the eight shades in which his shirts were available. I took the easy way out and had Vanraj Bhatia write me a piece of music to which a beautiful blonde could do the dance of the seven veils with the fabrics. (The eighth shade was wrapped around her head, poor thing.) And all this in one five-hour shoot, through the day, at the Taj. It was all a bit brainless but it was frantic fun and it kept me in pin money.

The client?

'Her bodice must be glistening,' he said. 'Glistening.'

So I got her a bodice made of metal scales. It glistened.

~

In 1965, I was suddenly told that *A Certain Childhood* was being sent to the Leipzig International Film Festival. When I arrived in Leipzig, I found that the theme of the festival was peace. Among a whole bunch of films about war and peace, I wasn't sure what my film on children with learning disabilities was doing, but it was probably the only peaceful thing the government could find to send.

From Leipzig I went to Paris, invited by Claude Nedjar, one of the big French producers. I had assisted Jacques Brissot when he was shooting the Pune and Bombay legs of *India: Culture for a Few Rupees*, a documentary. I had taken the unit to Pune to the ashram of B.K.S. Iyengar, under whom I had studied yoga. The film had been initiated by Pierre Schaeffer, head of the Department of Research of French TV. It was supposed to be a scathing attack on tourists who go to other countries looking for *la différance* and then find fault with the country because it is different. The cultural attaché of the Indian embassy had got wind of the documentary and wanted to see it first. Schaeffer and Nedjar wanted me to read it and make an educated guess about what would upset the government of India in the person of the cultural attaché. With my red pencil, I underlined the sections in which blue-rinsed Belgian ladies and grizzled German pensioners expressed their disgust at diseased people begging in the street, the pot-bellied children and the filth of Benares.

'But you do see, Madame Leela, this is not what we say,' said Schaeffer worriedly. 'We are mocking these people for not understanding poverty and wanting the world to be made in the image of their homes.'

'I can see that,' I said. 'But will the attaché?'

The attaché responded exactly as I expected. He said he would advise the government of India to ban the film. He also suggested that the government might feel less cooperative on future projects.

Schaeffer listened with the utmost politeness and then decided that it would be rather a pity if the film was to be banned in India, but he was not going to alter it. He then asked me if I had any other ideas for future films.

'To be made in India?' I asked.

'Indeed,' he replied.

I thought of the great travellers like Fahien and Hiuen Tsang. I thought of the women of Asansol whose husbands faced hell each day in the coal mines. I thought of the water problems that India was facing. I thought of the maharajas of India and wondered what Peter Ustinov would make of them.

Schaeffer loved all our ideas. He wanted me to be executive producer on all four films, but my first challenge was to get the government of India to give the team visas. When I returned to Bombay, I was told that I would have to get the finance minister, Morarji Desai's approval. I could not imagine why the finance ministry would have to be involved, but I had dealt with Indian bureaucracy long enough to know that it was not mine to reason why. Morarjibhai was in Nepal and when I finally got through to him, he said he would take a look at the papers when he got back.

Claude Nedjar came with me to meet him, when he agreed to meet us, many months later. He had entered the country on a tourist visa, since the government was not giving out any business visas to this bunch of French filmmakers. We flew into the most terrible pea-souper of a fog in Delhi. Outside my window, I could see the plane jettisoning fuel. Claude suddenly turned to me and straightened his tie.

'I shall now pray,' he said.

I thought it rather wonderful that he should want to meet his maker with the knot of his tie up against his neck. But we did land and we did get to see Morarji Desai. He put us through a series of odd questions—'Who is Peter Ustinov?' 'What does he want with the princes?' 'Who are these Chinese persons, Fahien and Hiuen Tsang?'—and finally agreed.

But that wasn't where it ended.

I had spent three years working on these films when suddenly the Ministry of External Affairs got into the act. In 1969, when the crews were ready to leave for India, they refused their visas at the very last moment. That was the straw that broke the back of Nedjar's tolerance. He decided that it was not possible to work with the Indian government.

He did send me some French francs and gave me copyright on all that I had written, but it was cold comfort.

~

And then I made my potty film.

By the end of the 1950s, thousands of Punjabis were migrating to London. They were truly fresh off the farms and like all Indian farmers, they were used to squatting in the fields. This worked fairly well among the bright sunbursts of mustard flowers, but it wasn't quite as effective if you tried it in the early morning on a flight to London.

'I have to fly jamaadaars down to London because no one will clean the airplanes,' said J.R.D. Tata to me and Bobby Kooka. 'And they get tiddly on the flight and don't clean the airplanes either. Leela, will you make a film to show them how to use the toilets on the planes? And while you're doing it, can you also include a message about the middlemen? They should know that they can walk into one of our offices and book a ticket without paying a middleman.'

It seemed like an odd sort of challenge. We would have to make a film that did not condescend to those encountering the new technologies of an alien culture. I thought it would be nice if we could use a little girl as the central character, a little girl on her way from India to England. All children must feel that they are encountering an alien culture as they grow up, moving from the honesty of their own responses to the decorum of what is considered polite. By using a child, we would not be offending the people who were watching the film, for in all cultures, children are meant to learn. If the learning rubs off on adults, they can always pretend that they knew all about sitting on a bowl and flushing a toilet.

But to get that, we had to start in the Punjab and it was a scalding summer among the fields. It was so hot I had prickly heat in my hair. The loo was blowing, (yes, yes, I can see the possibilities but I'm resisting), a hot gritty rush of air from the deserts of western India. I had asked a doctor friend what to do and he advised me to immerse my arms right up to the armpits in water. So I'd slip my arms into a trough and wait for the next shot. I did ask if the buffaloes would mind a foreign body in their drinking water. There were huge Punjabi guffaws at this. They smacked each other about, laughing. Maybe they were making jokes at my expense. Maybe they were imagining the buffaloes complaining, 'Farmer, there's a filmmaker in my drinking water.'

Every day, I would come back and sit in a bathtub full of water. I had the only room with any air-conditioning, but that was because it also housed the film and that needed to stay cool. People can manage the heat but Eastman colour film in those days? It needed delicate handling and cool air.

The room had obscene ashtrays with images of women high kicking on them. I had to get them to clear those out.

'We thought you'd like them since they're women,' the manager protested.

'You may take them away.' I said.

He seemed a little peeved.

Every day, I would set out at five in the morning to fetch Munni, who was playing the little girl in our film. The excitement of acting in a film soon faded and we had quite a few tantrums. One morning, for instance, Munni decided that she wanted make-up. A little girl from a village with make-up? It was absurd but Munni was not to be deterred. So I worked industriously on her face, dusting it with this and wiping it off again, painting it with that and then cleaning it off again and then presented her with a mirror. She pouted at herself, quite entranced.

Munni enjoyed her spell on the toilet, which we shot at the Air India office at Connaught Place. She liked the toilet paper too and began to pull out huge ribbons of it. She didn't want to get off the potty after that. And when she finally flushed the toilet, she stared mesmerised at the swirling water and then turned to the camera to ask puzzled, 'But where does it all go?'

Despite the heat, despite being up to my armpits in buffalo spit, I enjoyed making the twenty-minute film. Zafar Hai seemed unable to make up his mind about anything in time. S.R. Rao, the cameraman would ask me, 'How long is he going to take to make up his mind?'

Zafar overheard once and replied, 'I was just wondering . . .'

Rao replied, 'Wonder all you want but wonder fast. The sun isn't going to wait for you.'

For all her tantrums, Munni was a natural and she seemed delighted at her success at flushing the toilet. J.R.D. was delighted too and the jamaadaars stopped flying to London.

~

The United Nations Development Project sent Dom to India to make films for SITE, the pilot programme that came before television was launched in India. We returned to Delhi from New York in 1973. He was supposed to write the films and then get the government of India to fund them for him. Films Division was an underfunded, understaffed department and the staff weren't quite sure how to deal with a request such as Dom's. They were accustomed to the notion of commissioning someone to make a film, but they had no idea how to deal with a UN body commissioning a poet to make a film and then asking them to foot the bill.

We met I.K. Gujral who was the Information and Broadcasting minister. He was very charming but he said that the ministry had no money. And so we decided that we would try and go it alone. There were two films whose synopses Dom and I had written. The first one was on the mud-workers of Paharganj, *kumbhars* who also worked as undertakers and lived on practically nothing. For this one, I called Sukhdev Singh, who declared that he would work for free, his team would work for free and he would bring his own stock. He was a generous Punjabi and I was delighted when he addressed my husband as Dom Singh. Dom did not quite know how to respond to that, but when I explained that Singh came from *sinh*, the lion, he grew to like the appellation. They became great friends too.

The last schedule of the film was somewhere in Haryana, in a kumbhar village. On the penultimate day, Sukhi decided that the government needed to be needled a little. So he went to the manager of the government resort where we were staying and announced that a wedding party, a *baraat*, was expected that evening. He, Sukhi, was the host of the *baraat* and he expected to feed them as befit the guests of a wedding. The staff bustled about all day, getting into the spirit of a wedding. In the evening, everyone who had been involved in the film, from the crew to the kumbhars came to dine.

The bill came to several thousands, a considerable sum in the 1970s. Sukhi took a look at it and then signed it in a lordly fashion. Then he handed it to Dom.

'Dom Singh, give this to the bloody government,' he roared, his bonhomie powered by generous libations of rum.

The lion began to look a little green about the gills, if I may mix my zoological metaphors. Dom knew that the government was not going to pay a bill that large. He was right. I paid it.

The other film was called *A Profile in Courage* and we had Ram Mohan to direct it. He had worked on the titles of my other films and on the storyboard of my Terene commercial. He too agreed to work for free. The film was on Major Hari Singh Ahluwalia, one of the first men on Mount Everest. He had been shot in the spine by a sniper and had been rendered a quadriplegic. However, that had not slowed him down. He founded the Indian Spinal Injuries Centre in New Delhi and his resilience simply shone out of him.

~

Some time ago, Fabien Stillman came to see me. He was doing research on Louis Malle and he wanted to find out how the team had operated. Malle was making a series on India—what would eventually come to be called *L'Inde Phantome* or *Phantom India*. It was an extremely dangerous experiment since he was travelling across the country with no script, no plan, and only a single cameraman and a single sound recordist as his team. But when the cameraman is Etienne Becker—whose father was Renoir's cinematographer—and when the sound recordist is Jean-Claude Laurieux, this fool-hardy mission sounds less impossible.

When they arrived in India, I presume the French Embassy asked them what help they needed. Later, Malle told me that he had asked for someone who understood something about India, something about cinema, who knew a local language, but also knew French because his team members understood no English. They came up with my name.

Malle had a 16mm camera. He never used the viewfinder. He used his eyes. He left his cameraman to do what he had to do. They had a symbiotic relationship, sharing a complete understanding. He did not pontificate but he let Tinou, as Etienne was known, capture the atmosphere and he told Laurieux what he wanted and left him to figure it out.

I remember him telling me, between puffs of his black cheroots from Kerala, 'I don't have a script. It would be presumptuous of me to have one. India will speak for itself. It will write the script for me.'

We went to shoot at the temple of Vajradevi at Vajreshwari,

about ninety kilometres from the city, and famous for its hot springs. Today, the growing city seems to have surged right up to the steps of the temple but in those days, it was quite a trek and you prepared for it in advance, checking the tyres and stocking up on boiled water.

When we arrived, it seemed like we would never get to shoot. The devotees at the temple peered curiously at this team of French men, peered at their camera, peered straight into the lens. This disconcerted the team because it was not the cinéma-vérité they were looking for. Tinou was growing exasperated. I tried to explain that looking at someone is not quite as much of a crime in India as it is in Europe. I also tried to explain that Indian villagers were not very likely to encounter a French film crew in the ordinary course of their lives.

'Imagine a tiger wandering through Paris,' I said. 'That is the effect.'

He calmed down a little. Call a man a predatory beast and it always has a soothing effect. But it wasn't helping him film. Finally, I went up to someone who looked like a matron, a woman in charge.

'The foreigners are here to show the world how devout Indians are,' I said. 'And if people look at them, the world will think we do not pay attention to God, when someone comes near us with a camera.'

'And the world would be right,' she said and barked out a series of commands. Suddenly all eyes were to the front and the shooting proceeded.

The next day Malle asked, 'Do you know a space in Bombay, an isolated space, something that talks about its past, something that might remind us of the village it was?' I immediately thought about Banganga, the little temple tank on Malabar Hill.

He loved it when he saw it and did some shots. He had a great sense of music and explained an idea in his head. It involved a singer with a coloratura voice and an old folk song. I looked through my telephone diary and found the number for the Rishi Valley School.

Principal Balasundaram's wife was my Vijayalakshmi akka. I had met her at an education camp organised by J. Krishnamurthi at the Rishi Valley School. I knew that she had a beautiful antique Saraswati veena in her possession and that her voice was an extraordinary one.

I called her and explained that Louis Malle wanted her to sing for a film of his, to provide a theme for his exploration of India. She made only one condition. She would not stay at a hotel but at our home. I assured her that we would be honoured. And she would not sing at a studio but in our home. I assured her that it would not be a problem. But Laurieux did not look delighted at the thought. If sound recordists could do it, they would turn off the entire world while filming a theme or an important song.

Three days later she arrived. And the problems began.

First of all, there were the crows. Tinou wanted the windows open so that the light would be natural. But when you let in the light, you let in the sound of crows as well.

They spent an awful lot of time settling the matter. Then they decided that they would have the windows closed but Mumbai's crows are not easily denied. More heated Gallic discussion. Then I told them that we could be sure that the crows would be silent around two in the morning.

All eyes turned to Vijayalakshmi akka. She nodded serenely. She would sing at two in the morning, but she would like me to be her audience. I was delighted.

We did a trial run. Jean-Claude had a huge EMI with an automatic mixer. But again, he wasn't happy with the resonance coming off the floor. Twenty Persian carpets, which my mother had bought at various times and places, were unrolled and they went down on to the floor.

Early that morning, when the crows finally settled down to sleep and the city was still, Vijayalakshmi akka sat down and tuned her Saraswati veena for a while. Then she began to sing and we were all transfixed. After a while, Malle asked if she could sing an old folk song, perhaps something she thought was the oldest folk song of south India . . .

She sang again. And then she retired to bed. She did not eat and so none of us ate. Something spiritual seemed to have set in.

The next morning, Malle said to me, '*Avec une femme de cette dignité, je crois que nous ne pourrons pas demander qu'est-ce qu'on paie.*'

He was right, of course. She would not have dreamt of asking for payment. He could not have dreamt of paying. How does one pay for magic?

~

Again, it was on returning to Mumbai in 1981 that Uncle Jeh (J.R.D. Tata) asked me to suggest some films that I could help make. He asked me if I would write a synopsis for a film on vocational training for those who were not suited for academic degrees, which was the hobby-horse of someone on the board at the Tatas. I did another about the elections and the problems attendant upon them. There was one about adoption and another about commercial sex workers and beggar women. But the one that they eventually funded was on the problems of the city we lived in, which then went by the name of Bombay.

Bhagwan Das Garga was to direct it. He was not a young man by that time and I worked on the research, the scene synopses, the script, the scene break-down and I did the interviews too.

The film was called *Bombay: A City At Stake*. When we gave it to the Films Division, they asked for another ninety prints because they wanted to show it in other metros as well. Since the funds allocated by the Tatas would not cover the cost of replication, Films Division made two other copies and ran those ragged.

There's a moral hidden there somewhere, but these days I am not sure a moral is going to do this city much good.

~

I would have loved to make more documentaries, even in India. I remember meeting the imposing Lady Ranu Mukherjee whose family ran the Asansol coal mines. I had heard something of the dreadful conditions of the coal miners there and I wanted to go and take a look. So in the middle of Calcutta's creamy bhadralok, I asked her if I could visit.

She fixed me with a gimlet eye. I tried my best to look demure. I think she knew I meant trouble but she gave me a letter saying I was to be given all possible assistance and armed with it, I set off for Asansol.

At the mines, I told the superintendent that I intended going down a shaft. He looked like he was going to lay an egg at the thought of a friend of Lady Mukherjee descending where only expendable labour went. But I insisted so he gave me a yellow helmet and we got into a glorified bucket. We went down into the mine where the men worked at the coalface and the women worked as a kind of human conveyor belt, carrying the coal that came up from the shafts. I began to understand why the ancients put hell underground. I began to understand the notion of the Stygian depths, which I had read about in Greek mythology. Even if it wasn't for the claustrophobic dark lit only by dim lamps, even if it wasn't for the peculiar smell of a grave that was everywhere, even if it wasn't for the thin black dust that got into everything and would eventually kill each one of these men, there was something inhuman and dreadful about the scene. Art, I thought, cannot get anywhere near reality. Nothing, not even the great savagery of Fritz Lang's *Metropolis*, had come close to this kind of horror.

Thanks to Lady Mukherjee's letter, I was allowed to go everywhere and talk to everyone. I sat with the women and we talked about their lives. I tried to dress as simply as possible, in Bengali cotton saris but I knew that it was not enough camouflage. Across a huge gap of cultures and expectations, we sat in the coal-scented, lamp-black dusk and talked about their lives. In the background, there was the constant cough of men suffering from emphysema, men grown prematurely old from spending their lives underground; in the foreground, these women cooking dinner, still at work. And in their eyes, hope.

'Can your film get us a dispensary?' one of them asked me.

'Where do you go when you are sick?' I asked.

The nearest dispensary was miles away. The sick man had to be loaded on to a bullock cart and taken there. Often there was no money for the cart and so husband and wife would walk, slowly, for nearly a day . . .

I returned to my dharmashala every night and I wept. And I wrote my script and I searched for money but none was coming. I try not to think of those fire-lit faces in the coal gloom and the hope that my film might bring change. I try very hard not to think about it. I try and I fail.

ELEVEN

Among the Naxalites

The idea must have seemed good on paper. Dom Moraes, the young poet who had won the prestigious Hawthornden Prize, would return to his city and the BBC would follow him around with a camera. It was to be called *Return of a Stranger* and it was to be produced by one of the BBC's senior-most producers, Tony de Lotbinière. At the same time, they would be shooting a film called *The Bewildered Giant*, which represented their view of India in 1969.

As they drove through Bombay, Tony outlined his ideas to Dom. Dom would revisit his childhood friends . . .

A look of consternation must have spread over Dom's face.

'You do have childhood friends, do you not?' I can imagine Tony asking. He was not what you might call a terribly patient man. He smoked Kerala cheroots as if he were committing the acts of violence that he was not allowing himself. But when they did not suffice . . . Dom told me that Tony had once kicked his butt, actually, literally, kicked his butt when, in a scene set on the sands of Goa, Dom hadn't risen as quickly as Tony wanted.

Their car, Dom told me later, was just then passing the Opera House. And across the road from it, there was a huge poster of me in profile.

'I know her,' he said, relieved.

And indeed he did. My father and Dom's father, Frank Moraes, had been friends. We had known each other since I was two and he, four. Dom was a quiet and introverted child. But we got along quite well.

I remember, for instance, my fourth birthday party. I had invited Dom because he was the only little boy I considered a friend. Aunt Beryl, his mother, explained that Dom would not come to my birthday party but he would like to celebrate it with chocolate cake on the next day at his house. And so I dutifully went over the next day with chocolate cake. Dom ate it and then settled down to read.

'Talk to me,' I insisted, making an early start.

But he wouldn't. There was a gramophone in his nursery and so I suggested, 'Why don't we play musical chairs?'

Dom looked up, 'You have to pay if you lose.'

I wasn't preparing to lose. Dom wasn't a physical child. I was. I danced, I rode, I played sports. Dom spent all his time reading. So I agreed that there would be a penalty and when Dom lost, I told him that he would have to carry all his books on his head and that I would get to order something I wanted to eat, for a change.

He threw a nasty little-boy sulk but I insisted on the penalty. I was a little more forceful then, for I have a vivid recollection of Dom trying to carry a pile of books on his head and failing.

Now he was back but our friendship had not been going well. In 1959, when he had come back to write *Gone Away*, the first volume of his autobiography, he had called me up.

'It's Dom here,' he said.

'Dommie,' I exclaimed. 'What's happened to your voice?'

'Nothing is the matter with my voice,' he said.

'Well, you sound like you have a hot potato in your mouth,' I said.

There was a moment of silence. Then he decided to ignore my forthright comments.

'I want you to help me to research the film industry in India.'

I would have been delighted to help, but there was no way I could manage since I was shooting a film. We were then living in Bandra, my mother and I, in the ground floor of a rented villa with a maid to look after us and a hen devoted to my mother. To get to Mohan Studio on time, I had to get up at five o'clock. And since the shot was never ready when I arrived—my idea of punctuality differed radically from the Hindi film industry's notion of it—I spent much of my day waiting. The rule of all shoots anywhere in the world: if shooting starts late, it will end late. And I was lucky if I returned home by eight o'clock, drained and fit for nothing except a light dinner and bed.

Dom was not very happy when I refused. But now I was the only friend he could latch on to, the only one who had any memories of him in the city of his birth. And fortunately, at that point, I did have some time.

Tony asked him about me and the more he heard about me, the more excited he got.

'She's half-Indian and half-French. You're an Indian genetically, but you seem like a brown Englishman,' he said to him. So his lead question to me, on camera, was, 'How do you position yourself?'

This was many years before identity politics became such an important issue and the notion of belonging became so public. I suppose refugees have always known how important it is to be able to belong somewhere, but the larger world at that time seemed to be less concerned about such matters. So I answered as best as I could.

'I'm between two stools,' I said. 'But I am not falling. I can understand the Europeans and I am at home in India. I can grow roots anywhere.'

'Me too,' said Dom and shut up.

Tony was a bit flummoxed. This was supposed to be a conversation in which Dom would explore what it meant to him to be brown, to be Indian, to be living in England. He was supposed to offer something more than that.

'What do you mean?' he asked.

'I agree with Leela,' he said. Tony ground his cheroot between his teeth but nothing more could be got out of Dom. It was always that way with Dom. He was uncomfortable with self-revelation when it was direct. He could write it, he could shape it into his poetry, but he could not talk about himself. Obviously, the film was going to be a lot more difficult than he had thought but that was none of my concern. I was going to see my children in Delhi so I called Frank who would have been hurt if I didn't call.

'Dom is here,' he said, 'I'll tell him to meet you.'

I was staying at the India International Centre so he came and sat there with his shy, mumbling face. I offered him a cup of tea and promised myself I would make no teasing remarks.

'I have no clothes,' he said after clearing his throat. 'I have one brown shoe and one black shoe. I have three shirts but none of them have buttons. My tweed coat doesn't match my trousers.'

'I'll do your shopping for you,' I said.

'I have twenty pounds,' he said.

'Please forget it. I'll do it for you because you're my friend. You can pay me later.'

'It's not about shopping. Will you marry me?'

'Of course,' I said, feeling sorry for him.

He told Frank who wept, happily. Or so Dom told me.

'I suppose I must ask your father,' he said. I couldn't believe that a Bohemian poet with a Soho past could be so old-fashioned.

'You do not have to do any such thing. It's my business and yours,' I told him.

But as a pucca Brit, he felt he had to make it right. Later one evening, my father told me about it as he played a chess game against himself. I could play, he had taught me, but he found me unsatisfying as an opponent. 'You never attack,' he said to me once, 'you are always on the defensive.'

Prescient words, perhaps.

As he considered his next move, he told me what had happened when Dom had taken him to the Harbour Bar at the Taj Mahal Hotel.

'He actually asked for your hand in marriage,' said my father.

'Well, that was rather the point.'

'Yes, but I thought he might be a little more experimental in his use of the language,' said my father, claiming a white pawn.

'What did you say?'

'I told him that I would not let my daughter marry a man who mumbled,' said my father, claiming a black pawn.

'Daddy!'

'Of course, I said that he was welcome to have you if he wanted you.'

'Daddy!'

'I said it was your life and we had always let you decide for yourself.'

This was true.

'And I said that if you wanted to marry someone who was so scruffy . . .'

'He has always been a little scruffy,' I replied loftily. 'It has to do with the life of the mind . . .'

I could feel my father's eyes on me. He had a way of looking at you that punctured any pomposity. And it occurred to me that he was a man who had, as much as Dom, lived the life of the mind and yet he wasn't scruffy. Not flashy, of course, but never scruffy either.

'Scruffy is as scruffy does,' I said.

'It is always good to be loyal,' said my father, checkmating himself, 'But it is no good trying to defend the indefensible.'

~

The BBC team with which Dom was working then went on to Calcutta to shoot some sequences with the Naxalites. Dom called up a little later.

'Come and join us,' he said, affable and friendly. I suppose I should have smelt a rat. I suppose I should have smelt a huge decomposing rat. There was Dom with a whole bunch of men, all booze buddies together, and suddenly he remembers his fiancée, Leela?

When I arrived, it became apparent that the team was expecting Dom to be their local guide, their informant, their line producer, everything rolled into one. I don't know whether this was part of their agreement but the general feeling I got was that Dom had let down the side. The clock was ticking and the crew was beginning to get restive.

The first thing they wanted was a real live Naxalite. I was told that the crew had spent several bootless days chasing Monodeep Sen, supposed to be one of the most charismatic leaders. I have always believed that if you ask as many people as possible, someone will know a way to help you. And so I talked to as many people as I could. I even called Police Commissioner Mitra. The crew laughed at me. 'If they knew where the Naxalites were, surely they would have gone and arrested them,' they said. But I have always felt that the police in India know a lot more than they let on and it was worth taking a chance.

Finally, someone told me that Monodeep Sen was always holding court at the Calcutta University canteen. I went there and began asking around. On the general principle that charismatic political figures generally attract the best-looking girls, I asked a doe-eyed Bengali tigress where I could find Monodeep.

'Behind that bush,' she said.

I thought she was being facetious but when I went around the bush, there was a figure in a huge swathe of shawl.

'Monodeep Sen?' I asked.

He inclined his head. I explained that I was there on behalf of the BBC, which would like to interview him. I thought he would swear at me for being the lackey of an imperialist corporation or something like that but he looked quite flattered.

'I shall be in the canteen tomorrow at ten,' he said.

And so we betook ourselves, camera and crew to a typical college canteen which smelt of over-brewed tea and oil that had been abused by repeated use. There was graffiti on the walls but it wasn't quite the standard-issue scribbles of adolescents. 'Death to the zamindar' read one. 'Power to the peasant' read another and of course, 'Power flows through the barrel of the gun' all in red, dripping ersatz blood.

When Monodeep saw the camera crew arrive, he leapt on to the table and made an impassioned speech. I couldn't help thinking of Franz Fanon's acute observation, 'Fervour is the weapon of choice of the impotent,' as he rattled on and on. When he had finished, he leapt off the table and threw himself into a chair. He shot up again with a sharp yelp of agony.

'What happened?' I asked.

'My piles,' said the brave revolutionary, clutching his derrière.

'A sacrifice for the cause?' I suggested.

'Yes, I have spent hours sitting on rocks while my comrades went about killing the enemies of the farmer and the worker,' he said.

After the interview, Monodeep said that he would like a fruit juice at the Grand Hotel. He thought that if he sat between Dom and me in the car, he would be seen by the police and arrested. Just as we were leaving, a horde of students arrived, chanting slogans. They did not want Monodeep to talk to the imperialist lackey dogs and they wanted to smash the equipment, which was in the dicky of the car. But we got out of there just in time with Monodeep on the floor of the Ambassador. We smuggled him through the back door of the hotel. But as Monodeep drank his orange juice, there was a knock on the door.

I opened it to find the Police Commissioner outside.

'Ah, Monodeep,' he said quite politely.

The brave revolutionary paled.

'Don't worry,' said the Police Commissioner, still polite, 'I'm not here to arrest you.'

'I think I shall leave,' said the brave revolutionary and began to creep out.

'You can leave by the front door, you know,' said Mitra. 'Or would your Naxalite friends be horrified at the thought that you were dining in the hotels of reactionary elements?'

Monodeep scuttled off.

'I know his father, you see,' said the Police Commissioner later. 'Monodeep is quite harmless. He does not kill. He only keeps watch.'

Several years later, the *New York Times Sunday Magazine* commissioned Dom to do a series on the Naxalites. I rounded up some local journalists to help him. I was keen on meeting a real Naxalite this time, not just a speech-making stone-sitter. And so it was arranged that we meet a young man trained in chemistry and the making of explosives.

'He will only meet you because he has heard of your father,' said the man who made contact. And so we went off into the middle of old Calcutta to meet a maker of bombs.

I introduced Dom to the young scientist.

'Lal Salaam,' he said, waving his fist.

'How d'ye do.' asked Dom, proffering a British paw.

'He is an imperialist dog, I will not talk to him,' snarled the anarchist. 'But I will talk to you for Dr Naidu is a true communist.'

I could have told him that my father had never been a member of the communist party but it was not the time for fine distinctions. The young man began to talk. He had made many bombs, he told us. He had no idea how many people he had killed. But each bomb came back to haunt him. Every dream he had, he said, ended with people exploding. 'Whatever kind of dream it is, they explode,' he said.

'Why don't you stop?'

'Because I cannot. If I stop, then the faces of the peasants haunt me.'

'Is there no other way?'

'Other ways have been tried for hundreds of years and they have failed,' he said but I thought I could hear his despair. This was supposed to have been the ultimate solution. Power was supposed to flow from the barrel of their guns. But killing people had not empowered many villagers. It had simply brought the wrath of the state down upon them. I do not hold with all the easy rhetoric about the finest flower of that generation and all the rest of it. But I believe I saw honesty in that young man's eyes. Like all terrorists, he believed in what he was doing. Like all terrorists, he had no future and so he substituted his faith for his future. But he could not control his dreams.

We went next to the police station to see the work of the young man's hands. In a bucket of water lay something that looked a bit like a bowling ball.

'What's in it?' Dom wanted to know.

'Cow dung and shrapnel,' said the police officer.

I picked it up to get a closer look and immediately a hush fell upon the place.

'Put it down very carefully, back into the bucket,' said the police officer. I did so. When it went back into the water, everyone seemed to unfreeze. 'What are you doing, Madam? It could still have gone off.'

The Naxalites had called for a bandh and one of the journalists said that it would be a great time for us to go out and get a feel of a city under siege. Dom didn't want me to go along, but I insisted and we wandered around a quiet city. Our driver drove slowly, stopping for every football that the children kicked across our path.

'Who knows?' he asked rhetorically. 'It may look like a football but it may well be something else altogether.'

We wandered a little too successfully for eventually we were lost. I got out of the car and went to ask a policeman. Just then a series of thumps began. I realized that someone was shooting and the police were returning fire. But I was halfway to the policeman already so I ploughed on.

'Can you tell me the way back to the Park Hotel?' I asked.

The policeman looked a little dazed. It took him a moment or two to put his thoughts in order and get the words out. Needless to say, we got back safely. Needless to say because if we hadn't, I would hardly be here to tell my tale.

When we returned to our hotel room, there was Police Commissioner Mitra who seemed to be a bit annoyed.

'Did you want your head blown off?' he demanded. I took this for a rhetorical question and stayed silent.

'Perhaps you could explain it to her,' said Dom acidly. 'I have failed.'

I let them rant on and on. I have tried to live my life as a feminist would, in that I demand to be treated equally. This demand, to me, means not just equal rights but an equal share in any danger we may face.

~

Years later, when we passed through Calcutta on our journey around the world for *A Matter of People*, Dom's book on the population crisis, I suggested we look up our old friend, the Police Commissioner.

He was delighted to hear from us and came over.

Something had been nagging me for a while. I made bold enough to ask Mitra how he seemed to know where we were, who we had met, how I had 'risked' my life.

'We had you followed around,' he said. 'It was our duty.'

'What happened to Monodeep Sen?' I asked him.

'Oh, he joined his father's business,' I was told.

I did not ask what happened to the maker of bombs. I think I knew.

TWELVE

Caution: Leila Khaled Is Coming

I have worked all my life. I began working at the age of eighteen and I had always paid my way. Almost as soon as we got married in 1971, Dom left India to go to Hong Kong where he was to be editor of the *Asia Magazine*. Although I was tagging along with him, I could not spend my time doing nothing.

So I went out to look for work in Hong Kong. I applied to the Hong Kong government television station, Dinsi Dintoi. After a written examination, I was invited to a viva voce. It was a panel of red-faced colonial types, each one an impressively stuffed shirt.

'How would you report the students' agitation?' one of them asked me.

'I would report both sides,' I said. 'I would give the government and the students equal opportunity to express their views. Or to make fools of themselves.'

When I told my friends what I had said, they predicted that I had shot myself in the foot. That was no way to get a job in a government-funded organisation, they said. A couple of months passed and I began to believe them. But then I received another letter saying that I was hired.

Michael Kay, the production controller, took an instant dislike to me. I don't think I ever did anything to deserve it but once I was hired, he had notices put up saying, 'Beware: Leila Khaled is on her way.' Leila Khaled was the name of a Palestinian terrorist, which must have seemed very funny to him. He may well have been an intelligent man but he had so many chips on his shoulder that they negated his intelligence. He had had a three-month course at the BBC in London, and it had gone to his head. And through it. He wanted me to fail so badly that I decided that I would fight.

For my first assignment, in the Chinese Section, he told me that I should try and film a song, an old Mandarin song, he said.

'I don't know any Mandarin,' I protested.

'But you do know music,' he said.

I did. I went to the library—they had a good collection of songs and I sat down and I listened to hundreds until I found one I could respond to. It was a ballad that told the story of a boy who was forced to sell his horse because of a famine.

'Go ahead,' Kay said. 'Film it.'

That was when I realised that I would need a horse and a rider and if we were going to be realistic, some place in Hong Kong that didn't look like it belonged to the twentieth century.

Run Run Shaw was the man who had the finest stables in Hong Kong so I called him and asked for a horse, a slim horse that might look like it had been through a famine. Then I drove around Hong Kong until I found a cove, a beach that looked remote. Next step? A Chinese boy who could ride bareback and we were all set.

On the day before the shoot, Kay asked me what was happening. I told him what I was doing. His face clouded over until I told him my location. Then it brightened magically.

'That's far away from anywhere,' he crowed.

'Well, it is a period piece . . .'

'And how do you plan to feed your crew?'

I must say I hadn't thought about that because production companies generally provide for the crew's food. Like any army, a film crew also marches on its stomach. I had planned on taking carrots and sugar cubes for the horse but I hadn't planned on the people. I mentioned it to Dom in passing even as I was making arrangements for some Chinese food to be delivered there.

The next day, we were working with a horse that didn't want to go into the water and a little boy who was finding it hard to stop hamming and grinning for the camera. In the middle of this, I was rather surprised when Dom arrived at the shoot with some huge cardboard boxes.

'Here,' he announced grandly. 'Food for the hungry.'

I opened the boxes and found pâté sandwiches and smoked salmon.

'Where did you get this from?'

'The Peninsula Hotel,' said Dom airily. He then handed me an astronomical bill. I could imagine Kay's face if I were to present it to him and so, with a sinking heart, I decided that I would have to pay it myself. Meanwhile, the distributor of gourmet largesse found himself a rock and began to drink the cold beer he'd provided for himself. The Chinese crew approached the salmon and the pâté with some suspicion but they wolfed the sandwiches down eventually.

Very pleased with himself, Dom pointed out a sampan going off into the sunset. We used it as the last scene in which the boy must bid farewell to the horse. It came off so well that Kay had to suffer the odium of having the two private channels calling and saying that it was beautiful. (The sampan scene in particular found favour. An image of it sailing into the sunset is an auspicious omen to the Chinese.) Kay had expected me to fail because film wisdom holds that shooting with children or with animals is a nightmare. I hadn't heard of the dictum and in my ignorance, I had chosen a subject that had both. Kay must have thought I had played straight into his hands.

That didn't stop him trying again. General Romulo of the Philippines arrived with a dance troupe. Kay assigned me a single camera to shoot the dancers, even as they were performing for an elite audience at the Eagle's Nest restaurant in the Hilton. This meant that we weren't supposed to get in the way and still shoot dance, which is always a fairly strenuous job anyway. I devised a sign language and the cameraman Chen and I spent most of our time crouched in between tables, scuttling here and there. He almost went cross-eyed, trying to keep me in his line of sight for directions while still keeping the dancers in focus. Again, we pulled it off. And again Kay fumed and raged to himself.

I checked the manifests later and found that he could easily have assigned us the three cameras I had requisitioned.

I must say these successes would not have been half as satisfying had I not been working against Kay's freight of animus. Later, Dom interviewed Romulo in his hotel suite. For some peculiar reason, the hotel had decided that the general would be delighted if they added a huge replica of a piña hut built entirely of chocolate in his suite. I don't know why they did this; perhaps it was simply because they could. But there it was and after the interview which went quite well, the sound man backed into the hut and knocked it over.

In his panic, he began to rampage about, stamping the chocolate into the green carpet. Romulo was vastly amused.

'Perhaps they will now take it away,' he said.

~

Dom very rarely cracked a joke. He was called Dom Morose or Dumb Moraes at Oxford. As anyone who has read either of their travelogues to India knows, Ved Mehta was in Oxford with him. When he came to India, Ved wanted to meet me. I find it odd when a man who says he is blind compliments me on my beautiful long hair, especially if he has not even touched it. When he repeated the compliment, on another occasion, I taxed him with it. He said airily, 'I have a sixth sense for these things.'

I thought he wanted to talk to me about Indian cinema; I found out that he wanted to talk about himself. When he came to meet us in Hong Kong, Dom went to see him at his hotel, the Peninsula at Kowloon. Ved wanted to see the *Queen Elizabeth II,* which was docked in the harbour, but the ship burned down that day. He also said he wanted to meet the biggest Sindhi family in Hong Kong and so I got on to the telephone and made the necessary calls. The Sindhi family was typical of the nouveau riche all over the world. They had a yacht with a bar at which there was a fountain. This fountain was in the shape of a woman whose breasts flowed with the finest liquors. In the master bedroom of the house, there was a purple velveteen bedspread on a king-sized bed. Since the walls were also velveteen, this was quite outrageous but these aesthetic sins paled when you realised that the bed and the walls were decorated with ropes of pearls. The bathroom was orange and purple, accented with the red of cockroaches. The library was stocked with fake books that were all alcohol bottles.

Nothing was proportionate, nothing in good taste, nothing beautiful. The food was ordinary in the extreme: tandoori chicken, potato chips and ice cream. Ved enjoyed all this because it was exactly the kind of material he wanted. I didn't.

~

Hong Kong, I found, had a peculiar take on Buddhism. By some strange reading of the Dhammapada, people refused to donate blood, not even to their own children. The Chinese Buddhists would not even part with nail parings or hair. This meant that children with Rh factor problems, who needed blood transfusions immediately, would simply die. It seemed a dreadful thing and a subject for a story of public interest.

I got permission from the Queen Elizabeth Hospital to position our camera outside the door of an operation theatre. We set up around six in the morning and waited. I didn't know what we could expect, I didn't know what would happen but somewhere outside on a road, a young man had an accident. He was brought to that very operation theatre. He was losing blood steadily and there was none to replace it.

We could all see the level of the blood in the bottle that was attached to his arm drop steadily.

'More blood,' shouted the surgeon. 'We need more blood.'

'There is no more blood,' said the matron.

The family, who had been contacted, arrived. They were in tears—they knew their son was about to die, they knew this and they refused to donate the blood that could have saved his life. As he was being wheeled into the theatre, he died. In front of the camera.

I still don't know what to make of this moment. I still haven't been able to understand it. At one level, those people loved their son. At another level, they believed they were doing the right thing by not giving him blood. As for me, I was doing my dharma as a documentary filmmaker, pointing my camera at his dying face. The matron sat down on the bench next to me.

'We had four bottles of his blood type,' she said. 'That was the last one.'

But it was not over.

The doctor in charge of newborns took me to see the children born with Rh factor problems. All babies are beautiful but Chinese babies are particularly winsome. They lay in a row of such perfect prettiness, that your heart hurt a little.

'They may all die tonight if they do not get blood,' he said after a moment.

I did not cry. I could not cry. But for the next five hours, the cameraman and the sound recordist and I did not speak. There was nothing to say.

Then I thought, 'Well, there are people of other faiths in this city.'

So I went to the Hong Kong Cathedral and asked the priest to make an appeal for blood. In a makeshift camp outside the church, the armed forces, the firemen, the police, some expatriates, and some Chinese Christians donated blood.

When Kay watched the rushes, he wanted to excise the shots of the young man dying.

'Isn't that what "documentary" means? An attempt to document what happens?'

'Yes, but . . .'

'Then this happened. It happened in front of us. I will not cut it.'

'It will upset the Chinese.'

'Let it.'

He looked aghast at the idea of the media being disruptive. I felt there was little point in making documentaries if they did not cause some stir, did not make some impact, did not start some new thought processes and upset some old ones.

'Perhaps if we upset them into acts of charity, it might help save a few lives?' I asked.

The last vestiges of humanity must have remained in that stuffy fuddy-duddy for he left it alone. Inasmuch as I am proud of anything I have done, I was proud of my film on blood donation.

THIRTEEN

Breathless Victory

It was uncomfortable working with a man who did not like me but I could take it. I could even take the attitude of the Chinese to whom Indians were *acha*s (from the Sikh soldiers who would use the word '*achcha*' to indicate that all was well when on duty) and the white men were *gwailo*s (or red faces). But one day, I was told that 'Viewpoint', a talk show I was doing for the government-run Hong Kong television was 'going too far'.

When I had been given the assignment, I was delighted. It was a ten-minute talk show, Monday to Friday, and I was determined it would not be one that was filled with frilly ladies talking about their hydrangeas or an interview with the secretary of the local club.

'What do you mean, "going too far"?' I asked.

'You have been interviewing people on the black list,' I was told. One of my interviews had been with a lay missionary who had worked extensively in the Chinese ghetto. She had criticized the government's policies on housing for the Chinese, but she had never crossed the line into slander and had supported each one of her observations with facts and figures.

'I didn't even know there was a black list,' I said, my hackles rising.

But apparently there was one and all the other 'journalists' seemed to be aware of it and willing to pretend it did not exist. I could not. The Sikh accountant-general came to see me that afternoon.

'Leelaji,' he said, 'you must be wondering why you weren't confirmed when you were selected?'

Actually I was not wondering that at all. I have never understood these rococo hiring policies; either one is hired or one is not. I had been hired but apparently I had not been confirmed then.

'It is because they think your parents were communists.'

In those days of the Cold War, there could be no greater crime than being a communist. And verily, verily, the white man believed that the sins of the fathers should be visited on the sons. It did not matter that my father had never been a card-carrying member of the communist party or that my mother was a socialist, which is something completely different as both Nehru and Mao could have told these jokers. But to them anyone who wasn't completely sold on capitalism was against them. So investigations had to be made in five countries since my parents had lived in six cities: Paris, Geneva, London, New York, Mumbai and Delhi. It had taken them three months to satisfy themselves that I wasn't a fifth columnist or a red hat or something equally evil. But I was glad that I had still caused them trouble.

The next day, I resigned. I wrote a long, angry letter, telling them that I thought they were making a mockery of the notion of journalism.

After I left Dinsi Dintoi, one of my ex-colleagues in the English radio department rang me up.

'What are you up to, old girl?' he asked.

I was up to nothing and I told him so.

'Well, I have just the lark for you.'

Many members of the English staff were moonlighting for Hong Kong cinema, dubbing the action films that came spilling out of the studios. They needed a female voice for a warrior princess. Could I play the lady?

'Not quite the stuff, you're used to doing, I know,' he said, but that didn't bother me.

Since all this happened on the weekend, I took myself to a dubbing studio the size of a refrigerator and watched as a young Chinese woman rode up to the battlements, fought a battalion of soldiers, took a running leap at a ten-foot wall, fought another battalion of soldiers, took another running leap . . .

It did not look like there was much work to do. Finally, when she arrived at the topmost level of an impossibly multilevelled castle, she began to speak, reeling off what sounded like lines of poetry.

I looked down at my script.

'Victory,' I was supposed to cry.

But hold on, I thought, when a warrior princess slices off the heads of three evil guards with a single blow, surely she may be allowed a grunt? And when she arrived at the roof, surely she would be a little breathless. Could I be a little breathless?

I asked my ex-colleague who said, 'Darlin', you can be breathless or you can be breathy but we have to get this done by tomorrow evening or Run Run Shaw will have my guts for garters.'

Run Run Shaw? His was a name to contend with in Hong Kong in those days. He was all things to all people and some of those things were said to be downright unpleasant. It was rumoured, for instance, that he had once set up a fight to the finish between Jackie Chan and Bruce Lee on a deserted beach. And he made films that could be titled *Hand of Death* or *Five Fingers of Death* or *King Boxer* or *Iron Palm* or all of the above at the same time, as one film was.

I was not always the beautiful warrior princess with a vocabulary of grunts. Once I was the young girl who seemed to constantly need rescuing from a whole bunch of bad guys. I tried to inflect my dialogue, but it is very difficult to give 'Help, help' too many different interpretations.

We would work at it like slaves, barely coming up for breath. We weren't paid much—Shaw probably knew that much of the talent was moonlighting since he was believed to know everything that happened in Hong Kong—but he did send us hot towels and food. And the work was fun, it had something to do with film and I had some pin money at the end of it.

FOURTEEN

Travelling with Dom Moraes

When Dom was working on *A Matter of People*, I went with him. My self-respect would not allow me to be a supernumerary, an extra piece of luggage, but as it turned out, I would be his unpaid secretary making endless notes and translating his mumbled questions to puzzled people across the globe.

I remember Khushwant Singh writing somewhere that he once asked Indira Gandhi how she had managed to understand Dom's questions.

She replied, 'Oh, Leela translated.'

I did indeed, but it was not an easy job. While Mrs Gandhi seemed to be willing to cooperate in the writing of her biography, perhaps because her father's biography had been written by Dom's father, Frank Moraes, she seemed laconic to the point of being monosyllabic. Dom would ask a question. Mrs Gandhi would look at me. I would translate it into audible English. Mrs Gandhi would twitch an eye a little and say 'Yes' or 'No'. Dom would wait. So would I. The silence would extend into discomfort. Then he would rouse himself to ask his next question, again inaudible.

But there were times when he was quite, quite audible and that inevitably meant trouble. When we were passing through Kinshasa, Dom packed our bags. From time to time, he would take it upon himself to show me how things could be done. For instance, he would insist on shopping even if this was not always a good idea. Once, when he had been staying in paying guest accommodation in Chelsea, he told me that he had almost been evicted from the house, that the police had come in because the owner suspected that Dom had murdered someone and left the body behind to rot.

The suspicion was compounded by the fact that he was away at the time when the police broke down the door to get at the source of the foul odour. It was easily found: a huge piece of cod, rotting in the bathtub.

'The man at the shop told me I should soak it in water for a while,' he said.

'Didn't you ask how long that "while" should be?' I asked.

'It didn't occur to me,' he said.

'Why in the bathtub?' I asked.

'It was a huge piece and I didn't have any vessels large enough,' he said. Which meant the cod went into the bathtub, as all large pieces of fish that need to be soaked do in the world of men. Then of course, he had forgotten all about it. But this was the man who had once got into a bath with his clothes on so I suppose a forgotten fish was nothing extraordinary.

In Hong Kong, he decided that he would make us an omelette. This did not seem like something he could ruin very easily so Mimi, our Chinese maid, and I left him to it. When M le Chef had finished with his creation, he came out of the kitchen, poured himself a drink and ordered Mimi to dish up.

Mimi came out of the kitchen looking worried. When she served it I knew that something was the matter. The omelette was a strange shade of grey-green.

'What have you done?'

'Oh, I put in some port,' said Dom airily. He lived under the misapprehension that anything could be improved by the addition of alcohol in good measure. I went into the kitchen to check on the port wine. There was, I remembered, at least half a bottle.

When I came out of the kitchen, Dom was looking disconsolately at his omelette.

'It isn't very good,' he said.

'Oh Dommie,' I said and took a bite, determined to try and like it. Then I was forced to concede defeat.

'Perhaps we should have sandwiches,' I said. 'And Dommie, it is never a good idea to use half a bottle of port in an omelette.'

'I used eight eggs,' said Dom.

I looked at him.

'Eight *large* eggs,' he said.

On another occasion, when we were living in New York with forty-eight pots of African violets (don't ask) he invited friends over for dinner and insisted that he would cook. As far as I knew, his experiences in cooking lay in making a Poet's Stew.

This, according to Julian Mitchell, who was his contemporary at Oxford, was an impressive affair. Among the ingredients: leg of lamb marbled daintily with fat, grapes, artichoke hearts, fresh herbs, and two bottles of full Devonshire cream.

'This was rather expensive in the dead of winter,' said Julian ruefully, 'But Dom would have no substitutes. It was hot-house grapes, asparagus and imported artichoke hearts and good French wine.'

'Red wine?' I asked.

No, it wasn't red wine. It was white wine, because red would change the colour of the stew.

'The girls,' Dom often told me, 'would do the menial work. They would cut the onions and peel the garlic and such.'

Then after some herbs had been added—Dom was fuzzy about these details—it would be left to simmer as more wine and spirits were consumed by the visiting poets.

'Including Allen Ginsberg,' Dom said, 'that was the time he tried to touch Auden's feet.' Ginsberg failed to get Auden's blessings but he enjoyed the stew.

'How did it taste?' I asked Julian.

'The finishing touch to the stew was half a bottle of French cognac that would be poured over it and it would be flambéed,' said Julian. 'Since everyone would have been drinking all evening, do you think anyone cared what it tasted like?'

That day, I went out in the morning and spent the day in the quiet of The Cloisters. When I returned it was to find that my kitchen had been turned into a disaster area. I could not tell why we had run out of sugar and why the mixer was smoking like a funeral pyre in a rainstorm and the refrigerator was weeping all over the floor.

'What happened to the mixer?'

'It's not a very good piece of machinery, is it?' Dom asked.

'No, it is an extremely good piece of machinery when it is doing what it is supposed to be doing,' I retorted. 'I rather suspect it has been put to other uses.'

'Well, who would think it would be unable to grate nutmeg?' he asked rhetorically. 'And it made a frightful noise, Polly.'

I approached the cooking range. From a khaki-coloured soup, a few desolate chicken bones protruded. They looked like they had been worked over by a venomous axe murderer. That's why the chicken crossed the road: to get away from the axe murderer.

'I got the chicken cut up for me,' said Dom, as if absolving himself of avian felonies.

'Who cut that for you?' I asked.

'The pizza parlour down the road.'

I could not imagine why Dom had gone shopping at a pizza parlour for chicken.

'They put chicken on their pizzas, Polly,' he said condescendingly.

'Which is why they don't sell it to customers.'

'I persuaded him,' said Dom.

Later, I discovered that the persuasion had taken the form of fifty dollars, rather a princely sum in the 1970s. He had gone to the pizza parlour because he was loath to cut up a chicken.

I mopped up and dashed out to D'Agostino's to get the makings of a salad, some cold cuts and cheese for a cheese board.

Naresh Trehan, the cardiac surgeon, and his wife Madhu were our guests on that fateful evening. Dom presented his strange curry to all of us with the air of a magician producing a dodo from a hat. But he knew his food and it took only a bite for him to know what he had wrought. The sugar in place of the salt was the least of that curry's woes. But we didn't have to eat it and settled down to the salad and cold cuts and cheese.

At the end of the meal, Dom invited them back for his birthday. The Trehans began to look a little hunted.

'Don't worry,' he said, 'I'll get Leela to cook.'

They did come back and brought with them a pain d'épices, a honey cake made aromatic with spices. It was already sliced and one segment had 'Only for Dom' marked on it with icing sugar.

After the meal, Dom reached for his slice and bit into it. His face went a bit green. It was a slice that was laden with salt instead of sugar.

'There is much to be said,' I told him later, 'in leaving things to the experts.'

But our nation lives on the myth of the Renaissance Man, something the Bengalis took to their hearts and everyone else seemed to want to emulate. Obviously, that morning in Kinshasa, he was going to demonstrate his skill in The Correct Way to Pack a Case. From what I could make out, this meant throwing everything one can lay one's hands on into the suitcase, asking a passing person such as a conveniently placed spouse to sit upon it and then locking it and drinking a beer.

'There, Polly,' he said. 'That was quite easily done.'

It was indeed, if you didn't mind clean clothes dumped in with dirty clothes, and everything creased beyond recognition at the next stop. But when a man wants to show you how things are done, I have learnt, it is best to simply wait him out. Most of the time he will grow bored halfway through the job and the damage can then be undone. But Dom had finished this job and I was not allowed to touch the suitcase without suspicious questions.

I was glad to be leaving Kinshasa. Mr Miller, the Irishman in New York who checked over our accounts, warned me that it was the second most expensive city in the world.

'And the soldiers,' he said, 'Beware of anyone who wears a uniform. They are always ready to shoot. It won't take much to upset them enough to shoot your husband . . .'

As I contemplated early widowhood, he sighed deeply.

'. . . or you.'

When we arrived at the airport, Dom, buoyed by his success at instant packing, checked the luggage in. And we presented ourselves at the airport without our passports or our laissez-passer, an all-purpose document issued by the United Nations that was supposed to get us from country to country. Dom had packed it into the suitcase.

'Où sont vos passports?' asked the fat officer behind the counter. (Why are they always fat?)

'Dans le airplane,' said Dom, airing his mouldy French. 'Mais nous avons un laissez-passer.'

'Laissez-passer? Quel pays est-il?' asked the officer, who seemed to think it was a nation of some kind. I noticed that he was in uniform. And that he had a gun. Mr Miller's words did not seem very funny.

'Pas un pays,' Dom tried to explain that it was not a country and then collapsed. 'The United Nations.'

'Et qu'est-ce que c'est?' asked the officer, unimpressed. I found it hard to believe that he had not heard of the United Nations but he was probably simply responding to Dom's high-handedness. (He had a gun.) After all, *we* were at fault. (He had a gun.) *We* should have been apologizing for packing our papers in our luggage. (He had a gun.) Instead Dom lost his patience. It did not take much.

'What is this fucking bullshit?' he demanded of the air, of me, of the officer, of the fates.

'Moi, je ne parle pas l'Anglais mais je comprend le "fucking" et "bullshit",' snarled the officer, outraged. He seemed to be about to reach for his gun.

I jumped in to prevent the incarceration of two United Nations representatives and a possible international kerfuffle.

'Monsieur,' I said, 'He is not speaking to you. He is speaking to me. He always speaks to me like that.'

And I kicked Dom in the ankle. This made him growl further imprecations at me, which convinced the immigration officer that he was dealing with a lunatic.

'Cochon. Salaud,' he snarled. Then he looked at me. 'Pauvre petite.'

I suppose a good feminist would have resented such patriarchal pity but I just wanted to get on the plane. So when he waved us through, I grabbed Dom's arm and yanked him along.

'Next time, you pack,' said Dom as he closed his eyes and prepared to sleep off his exertions.

I took a very deep breath.

~

In the Philippines, Dom and I were invited to a dinner party in a mansion. An overenthusiastic maid had polished the granite stairs with Mansion Polish and three dinner guests slipped and fell in one night. One of them was me.

The local UNDP officer had a drunken surgeon staying with him and I was taken there. I suddenly felt like I was in the middle of a Graham Greene novel as he fumbled around, breathing clouds of raw whisky into my face.

'Nothing wrong with her,' he said, thumping me on the thigh and sending an arrow of pain down into my ankle. 'Good strong bones. Just a sprain.'

But the next day my foot was a balloon. Dom had to leave on the next lap of his trip so he left me behind. Chino Roces came to see me, bringing his wife Pachita with him. He was one of the best-known journalists of the Philippines and had valiantly fought the Marcos government's subversion of the Constitution. He now has a bridge and a street named after him in Manila. He also had an odd sense of humour.

'I shall tell everybody that Dom beats you,' he chortled. Then he wheeled me through the lobby of the hotel, saying, 'This is what her husband does to her.'

'Where are you taking me?' I asked.

'To the chap who tends the football team,' he said.

I tried to relax but another surreal experience was awaiting me. A tiny, rotund man looked at my foot and tut-tutted a bit. Then he announced that he couldn't quite tell what was wrong but he knew how to find out.

'When any of my footballers come in with a foot like this,' he indicated my foot which now looked like an alien life form surgically attached to me, 'I simply twist the foot right around.'

I tried not to squeak my horror at this.

'If they faint, it is a fracture. If they do not faint, it is a sprain.'

I wondered what had happened to the good old-fashioned X-ray. Surely Wilhelm Röntgen had not died of a carcinoma of the intestine for naught?

'Go ahead,' shouted Roces. 'She is a strong lady.'

I wished I could be treated like a fainting violet sometimes. It might be . . . a supernova of pain disrupted all thought processes.

'See,' said the physiotherapist from purgatory with a grin. 'It is only a sprain. Rub some horse liniment on it and you'll be fine.'

I was taking no pain killers and I was not about to subject myself to the burn of horse liniment. He also recommended two days of bed rest and dips in the hot springs, which didn't seem that bad. I decided that I would then go back to Bombay to be with my parents. Pachita gave me one of her delectable mango cream cakes for my parents.

'Make sure the security guards do not open the box at the airport,' she said. I have always made it a policy to cooperate with guards as far as is possible. So I opened the box when they asked me to.

'Ah Madame, a cake,' said one. 'But it might contain a bomb, might it not?'

And he plunged his finger into it, and scooped out a healthy chunk. When he had licked his finger clean, he waved me through to the next level of security. There, again, the box was lifted off my lap as I sat helplessly in the wheelchair and another searching finger investigated its luscious depths.

'For drugs, Madame,' said the guard.

When the third test began—I forget the excuse for this one—I abandoned the cake and simply flew home to rest for a bit.

After a couple of days, I flew out of Bombay again to Nairobi to join Dom. I hobbled along, mainly on one foot, making the best time I could, all the way through the Rift Valley, to the Victoria Lake. This, of course, is the land of the Masai, a naturally elegant people, who balance on one foot as they tend their flocks. Nothing like them to make you feel even clumsier as you hobble past. And there was nothing like the Indians settled there to make you feel ashamed. Whether it was the group of Indian businessmen swilling beer at the next table in the hotel at Lake Victoria or the Indian shopkeeper, they were all rude to the Africans, treating them with distaste and arrogance. But it was at Entebbe, from the window of an Air Afrique airplane, that I watched racism at its worst. I was looking out of the window of the aircraft as it emptied, when I saw our Belgian pilot kicking a worker.

Not metaphorically kicking but actually, literally kicking him.

'Monsieur,' I shrieked. 'Stop at once.'

He looked up.

'Would you care to fall out of the sky, Madame?' he asked politely.

'No, of course not.'

'Then I must kick these pigs or they will add water to the fuel and your plane will fall out of the sky before it lands.'

He went back to kicking his ground staff. I felt horribly inadequate.

Surely, there was some other way of convincing the workers not to endanger human lives without resorting to dehumanizing them? But then wherever I have travelled, men seem capable of contempt and inhumanity. The greater the difference between the man with the whip and the man with the scarred back, the greater the ease with which one can mistreat the other.

At Entebbe, a wonderful young man climbed aboard. He was wearing a boubou, one of those dramatic robes of many colours. He was with an assistant of some kind and both of them settled down in the seats in front of us. After we were airborne, the young man proceeded to take off his boubou. His assistant tried to remonstrate with him but to no avail.

'Give me my needle,' said the young man.

It became obvious that we had on board a drug addict who was quite far gone. He was administered his needle but it did not suffice.

There were two airhostesses, one Belgian and the other African. The Belgian airhostess walked past us and shrieked. The young man had taken off all his clothes. The African airhostess was called and handed the assistant a napkin which was duly spread across the young man's loins.

In a while, this went flying through the air. The young man was nude again. 'Give me my needle,' he insisted and once more, he was dosed.

For a while all was well and he allowed the assistant to drape the napkin so as to protect the modesty of those passing in the aisle. But again, the napkin was airborne and the protests began.

When we arrived at Kinshasa, we were the last to leave the airplane. I was hobbling and he was nude. He caught my eye. I smiled.

'What a lovely robe this is,' I said, much as I would to a child. 'I wish I could wear it.'

'It's my robe,' he said.

'No,' I pointed out. 'You're not wearing it.'

'I was going to,' he said.

The assistant bundled him into it.

'I want my needle,' he said.

'He will die, madame,' said the assistant to me. 'Explain it to him.'

On the runway, I could see a group of Africans, the young man's family, waiting for him.

'Gosh,' I said, 'Look, someone's family has come.'

The young man looked at the group on the runway. Then he scowled again.

'No, no, smile,' I said. 'What a nice smile you have.'

And so we got him to the door, urging him along like a child. At the door he stopped.

'I don't want to get off this plane,' he pouted. 'I've had so much fun on it.'

Sure, I thought, with those many needles . . .

When I managed to limp off the plane, Dom looked at my foot and said, 'Go and see a doctor.'

But there was no time. We were in Kinshasa only for a night, and had to fly to Gabon. There, we had an appointment with a minister and I was needed to make notes because he spoke French. And then we had to cross the Sahel Desert where Dom was supposed to be investigating the link between population growth and the march of the desert. We drove to a little settlement, only to find it deserted. No goats. No dogs. Nothing. Only the sand billowing endlessly around the skeletons of dead cattle. I walked around and suddenly through a door, banging in the hot sandy breeze, I saw what looked like a human form. I retraced my steps. It was a man.

I peered in.

'May I come in?' I asked, trying French.

'Please,' said the old man who was lying inside his hut. What I could see of his torso made him look like one of the Starving Buddhas of the Gandharva period. The village had emptied over time, he told me. Years of drought had taken everyone away but he was not going. He was the chief of his tribe and he was going to stay where his ancestors had lived and died. He had grown too weak to move. He could no longer hunt with the beautiful bow and arrow that hung above his head.

'But there is nothing left to hunt,' he sighed. 'Where have all the rabbits gone?'

Outside the hut, the sands stretched like a lunar landscape, barren and bare. It was difficult to think that it once supported human life, that it supported agriculture, that people had lived here.

'Monsieur le chef,' I said, for that is how one addresses a chief, 'How do you manage?'

The UNDP, he told me, sent him a baguette, a loaf of French bread that was more crust than crumb, every alternate day with a can of red beans and a canister of water. The canister of water was very low. He saw me looking at it.

'Are you thirsty?' he asked. 'You must drink.'

This was a man lying all alone in the middle of the desert, but he was still hospitable. It must have cost him much to offer me some of his ration of water but he did.

When we reached Dakar, Senegal, I did my best to raise hell with the UNDP. Three loaves of bread a week with just one tin of beans and not enough water to last a week? How was anyone to live on that much? Finally, I got them to agree to send something more by way of food and medical assistance.

At Dakar, I was asked if I would like to see the island of Gorée, which had once played an important role in the slave trade. It was here that the slaves were held before they were 'exported'.

The man who took me around was a historian and a scholar. He had spent his life looking into the dark heart of human misery but he was a gentle chap and as he showed me around the miserable quarters where the slaves were kept, where they were examined, where they were weighed, I could tell that he was still moved by the terrible iniquities that had been committed upon the innocent.

It is difficult to revisit even in my mind the horrors of that island. This was where they kept the men, this was where they kept the women, this was where the children were kept, this was where, sinisterly, it seemed, they kept the young girls. The slaves, who lived in chains, were fed once a day. Each would step up to a cauldron of gruel and each one had five minutes to eat before he was pushed back towards the cell. The walls were damp. Tuberculosis was rampant. Thousands must have died even before they were confined to holds and taken away. The way the human cargo was packed into the holds of the slave ships gave us the phrase 'packed like sardines'. The traders' quarters, though spartan, were paradise in comparison.

'It must be difficult to forgive Europe and America?' I asked.

'Oh Madame, history does not allow us to make enemies of other nations,' said the guide. 'It was the Africans who would sell members of other tribes into the slave trade. After a tribal war, they would take slaves as part of their booty. And when the Europeans came, they simply turned their booty into part of the commodity trade.'

～

In the evening, I finally went to a doctor.

This time I decided that I was going to be X-rayed and if anyone made any comments about strong bones, I would hit him first and thank him later. The doctor took an X-ray and declared that I had a fractured ankle.

'I could break the bone again,' he said cheerfully. 'But you have strong bones so we'll just let it heal.'

I didn't hit him but it was a near thing.

～

In Japan, there were some intriguing signboards in the Katsura Hotel.

'No Samurai allowed with Sord', one said.

'No suicide allowed', another read. Okay, I thought, I will try very hard.

'All windows seeled', read a third.

'No yam for breakfast'.

It seemed like a difficult way to live, but I thought I could manage. Then I realised that it was a typo and there would be no jam for breakfast. Or maybe ham. Or maybe there would be neither yam nor ham nor jam. Damn.

It would be difficult to make a list of all the things Dom hated because there would be so many of them. But museums were anathema. Whenever we were in any city together, I would head off to the museum and Dom would head off to the bar. In a way, it was a relief because I could take my time over the paintings or the sculptures or the implements of everyday lives of people. In a way, it was sad because one wants to turn around and share one's discoveries; one wants to say what one is feeling to someone who will understand. But between being lonely and being hurried, I'll take being lonely, thank you.

In Kyoto, a Japanese photographer who had a passion for whisky and a dislike for culture, accompanied Dom and me. In him, Dom found a soul mate. After all, when Dom was supposed to write about French tapestry and we visited Cluny and the tapestry room at the Louvre, where the greatest tapestries hang, the only thing that excited him was the image of a dog that had produced a turd, in one corner of the huge hunting scene depicting thousands of figures in a forest.

When I told them that I was off to see the world-famous collection of Kenzo screens at the Imperial Palace neither looked very excited. I knew that I was going alone again. The Imperial Palace was truly lovely and almost empty. There was one guard, bright and young, with a pleasant smile. I smiled back, which might have been a cultural mistake for he began to follow me through the dark rooms around the armoury. I began to walk faster and he speeded up too. The floors were designed so that no one could walk over them without a warning tinkle. And I could hear him tinkling after me. Finally, he called out to me so I stopped to confront him.

'Shake hand,' he said. I was so relieved that that was all he wanted, I forgot to use the oldest trick in the book: the namasté (folding your hands keeps you out of theirs). As soon as he took my hand, he began to pull me towards him. I broke free and I ran. Ballet, bharatanatyam and horse-riding have given me strong legs and I made good use of them, running until I got to a better-lit space. When I returned, there was Dom and the footling photographer.

'Now what's the matter?'

I told him.

'Serves you right,' said Dom.

'No one gets raped in Kyoto,' said the photographer, confirming my dim view of his intelligence.

But Japan had some moments of startling beauty at Kokedera, a Buddhist moss garden around the Saiho-ji Temple. There were a hundred and twenty different varieties of moss with colours that varied from the rich green velvet of Mumbai walls after the rains to a startling maroon and a deep aquamarine. It is one of the earliest gardens to have been designed in accordance with Zen thought and was designed by Muou Soseki, a thirteenth-century genius who designed many other such gardens throughout Japan. It is a *karesansui* garden, which means it has been designed to be viewed from a single location. You are supposed to sit down and begin looking and continue looking until you no longer see what you are seeing. I read a line of his poetry in translation somewhere:

When the mind is still
the floor where I sit
is endless space.

I loved Japan, the architectural detailing, the minimalism of art inspired by Zen and the music. Of course, I wanted to see Kabuki and Noh. Of course Dom didn't want to go, so I went alone and enjoyed the glorious excesses of ancient theatrical forms.

FIFTEEN

Translating Ionesco

Translation has always seemed to me to be not only an act of necessity but also one of sheer folly. To be cut off from other minds simply because of a difference in language seems unbearably grim and terribly unfair. On the other hand, an attempt to carry the meaning and the connotations of a phrase or an idiom across languages, cultures, time zones and space, seems to be an unbelievably heroic venture, one that is doomed, if not to failure, to always being a poor second, a shadow of the thing itself. I read somewhere that Yahuda Amichai, the great Israeli poet, compared reading a translation of a poem to kissing a woman through a veil. And the Iranians, a friend tells me, have a proverb which says that reading a translation is like looking at the wrong side of a carpet. I must say I have enjoyed these veiled kisses and upside-down carpets quite a lot but I have a small advantage in that I am bilingual. My thoughts sometimes occur to me in French and sometimes in English. I often find myself speaking the 'wrong' language, or appropriating a French word in the middle of English. Oddly, the reverse never happens. I don't need too many English words when I am speaking French but then perhaps that's the residual Française in me. After all, France must be the only country that has tried to ban English words like le jogging, le hamburger and le weekend by law!

After Dom finished the manuscript for *A Matter of People* and submitted it to the UNFPA, there was not much they had for a poet and journalist at large. And so they came up with an idea. Dom would ask twenty-five of the world's most important people in their respective fields of endeavour the question: 'What do you see as the quality of life, and what do you think it will become in the future?' The list contained people such as Heinrich Boll, Carlos Fuentes, Indira Gandhi, Eugène Ionesco, Margaret Mead, Yehudi Menuhin, Gloria Steinem and Buckminster Fuller. This was the book that came to be called *Voices for Life: Reflections on the Human Condition*.

It was a great idea but in the making of it, he ran into a couple of snags. One of the people that had been agreed upon was Eugène Ionesco, one of the greatest playwrights of the Theatre of the Absurd genre. I thought this was completely apposite even if the Theatre of the Absurd was about the insignificance of human existence. Most people believe that the Absurdists felt that communication had reached the level of Babel, that meaninglessness was all that lay behind the façade of human interaction but I have always thought otherwise. To begin with, if they allowed that belief to reach its logical conclusion, they would not have written at all—simply because to write needs an act of faith and to publish or to perform needs an act of trust in some community of communication. The Absurdists were not nihilists; by pointing out our failure to connect with each other, I believe that they were urging us to connect. By emphasising the non-linear, they sought to remind us that we still have the choice to allow for another way of living. By producing near meaningless conversations, they sought to challenge us into refining meaning.

And so Ionesco fit perfectly, according to me. Dom duly rang him up and after a few seconds, hung up disgruntled.

'He wanted to talk Froggy,' he said.

I did not think that a polite way to refer to the language of Racine and Valéry, but I held my peace and offered to call him.

Ionesco was charming and when I explained the project to him, he declared that he would willingly write for such a book. Ha, I thought, to myself. Take that, you nihilists. Here is the Big Daddy of the Absurdists agreeing to write about the value of human life.

'My theme is that life is like a circus, and that most of us are clowns,' he said. I told him that he could say what he wanted.

'I shall need two weeks,' he declared.

That was better than I had hoped.

'And I will write in French,' he said.

I told him that we would be delighted and that he should let us know if he had a translator of choice to whom we could send the piece when it was done.

'No, no,' he said, 'you translate it.'

I was rather overwhelmed by this, but two weeks later when the piece arrived and I read it, I found that it was easy because Ionesco had written it without flourishes, a *j'accuse* that indicted us all. It took me a week and when I finished, Dom read the piece with a look of growing dismay. He began to read out lines at random:

'"People lived yesterday and today exactly as they deserve to"? "To murder children has been a habit in mankind's history"? "Man is a social animal who cannot stand society"? "What is better? To be afraid of robbers and murderers or to be afraid of the police?" Polly, you were saying that his work was about the value of human life?'

'Suppose we read it another way,' I suggested. 'Suppose we read it as rhetoric. Suppose we read it as a challenge.'

Dom applied himself to the piece again.

'I suppose one could read it that way,' he said, although he looked doubtful. 'But what about the end of the piece?'

I took my translation from him and read it again: 'For us to reduce what is wrong with us to a minimum, we need competent administrators who have no ambition, resentment, or doctrines. As for a fair sharing of economic goods, we could suggest that it be left to programmers. But there again, it would not do much to our situation as creatures who will die or to our tragic existence.'

'It is pretty bleak but it is all true. As mortal beings, we are fated to die. And if that is the end, then all of us are tragedies and small changes are not likely to make much difference to that essential tragedy.'

'If all life ends in death, then all life is a tragedy. That's what he's saying.'

'Let's say he is saying all of this in complete good faith. Even so, I believe he fits into the book because we should have one voice that speaks for the meaninglessness of any attempt to escape our eventual fate.'

'Now that we've asked him, I don't suppose we can throw it out,' said Dom, morose.

One of the other authors we asked was the great French novelist and Poe biographer, Georges Walter. He too insisted that he would write in French and that I should translate his piece. Recently, I stumbled on a copy of *Voices for Life* given to me by a friend and re-read the piece. I remembered translating it, sitting up in bed in the Gramercy Park Hotel, wondering at the strange new world that Walter was conjuring up. Now, sitting in my bed in Colaba, more than three decades later, some of it is almost prophetic.

'If we find ourselves with too much power too soon, maybe it is time for us to learn how to use the toys we manipulate, to know that what contains the worst can also contain the best. The information media is sometimes like that huge machine a humorist conceived of, as big as a locomotive but, though full of cogs, pistons and bolts, only able to crack a hazelnut. If all too often communication conveys insignificant matters, it does happen that the publicity that goes with information brings out what was kept hidden and acts brutally as the voice of justice. When a paper has no other power than a fact whose truth it proclaims with obstinacy, with substantiating evidence, then it shows real strength. Television can inflict the face and words of a nitwit upon us; but it can also reveal the sincerity that goes with the face and words of a valuable man, and it can show up the impostors.'

I looked up from the book at the news channel that I had been watching and a parade of nitwits passed before my eyes.

~

I did not get paid for the translations. Since I was a woman working with my husband, the United Nations did not feel the need to pay me. Rafael Salas, the Secretary of the UNFPA, once said that my notebooks were all part of the archives at the United Nations.

'And it is most fortunate that you are wedded to M Moraes,' he said, with a hint of mischief. 'Or we would have had to pay you.'

Ouch, I thought.

I didn't say it, of course. I have always been rather bad about commercial matters and poor Dom was not much better.

But there were a couple of occasions on which I was paid for the translations I did. The first time was after *A Matter of People*. We were in New York when I got a call from Krishna Singh, who was the editor of the UN's film projects. He suggested that I do a simultaneous translation into English for twenty films that had been made for the International Year of Women. Each of the films had been made by an important director from the country and dealt with how women were faring in that country. The films were roughly from what is now called the Global South, from South America, Africa, South-east Asia and Asia.

I asked if I could sée the films first and later, I was glad that I did. The directors of all the films were supposed to be in the control room of the huge auditorium and they were supposed to be cueing me. Unfortunately, contact between the control room and the podium at which I was sitting broke down and I was suddenly left looking at films in languages as diverse as Swahili and Hindi without any cues. Of course, I could do the ones that were in English, French or Hindi, but what about Malay? Spanish was not such a problem but Portuguese?

I had a choice. I could run from the stage, shrieking that no one should be expected to do a job like that without working equipment or I could make an educated guess about when I should start and when I should stop. I didn't have much time to choose, mere seconds, and even before I had consciously come to a decision, I heard my own voice reading the first lines.

The next three hours or so—each of the twenty films was about ten minutes long—passed in a bit of a haze. I was trying desperately to remember what I had seen of the films and match them to the script in front of me. I was watching the screen intensely to follow the body language of the women speaking. A woman's shoulders rise slightly when she speaks to a camera and they return to normal when she has finished what she wants to say.

When it was over, I was thoroughly exhausted. Then suddenly, there was a bubble and gurgle and squeak of voices as the directors gathered around me on the stage. I studied their faces for signs that they were forming a lynch mob. But all was well; they merely wanted to congratulate me. When they had found themselves unable to communicate with me, they thought that all was lost. But I battled my way through it and Carillo Flores, Under-Secretary General of the UN, came up to say that I had done a good job of it.

Several years later, when I was in Delhi and Dom went off to Sri Lanka to do a story for *Stern* magazine, I found that I had forty-five rupees in our joint account in the bank. But then, *deus ex machina*, a formidable lady turned up at our doorstep and asked if I would do some simultaneous translation for an international seminar on World Free Press. One of the speakers was Eamon de Valera, president of Ireland, and co-owner of one of the Irish Press newspapers. He was going to speak in French. I agreed, assuming that a president would rarely allow himself the liberty of extempore speech. The best of them sound like they're making it up as they go along, but almost every word is devised by consultants and weighed by spin doctors. So I arrived at the Ashoka Hotel, and was seated in a cabin with headphones placed on my head.

'Where is my script?' I asked.

'There isn't one,' said a nervous young woman in a silk sari and too much perfume.

Before I could ask another question de Valera was off and I was too. He spoke simply, eloquently and while he did refer to Ireland, he only did so when it was apposite. His was the voice of the moderate, the man who has run a newspaper but has also run a nation. It was also the voice of a man who could speak for an hour at a time.

Later, he came up to thank me for my translation.

'Well done,' he said.

I was . . . I have been trying to figure out what I was. I don't think I was chuffed when Ionesco or Walter or de Valera thanked me for a good translation. I think I was grateful. There's a difference.

Yes. I was grateful.

~

Could it be the French side of me or was it that Hamburg in the winter of 1973 was truly depressing? It seemed grey and bleak and humourless. We were there to interview Günter Grass for *Voices for Life* and it was with relief that we drove out of the city and into the German countryside to Wevelsflatte where the author lived.

The young man who was our guide spoke poor penn'orth of English but when he discovered where we were headed, he began to look more and more discomfited. Finally, when we arrived, he refused to go into the house.

This made things difficult because he was supposed to be Dom's translator as well but he simply refused. Grass came out to find out what was going on. He invited the young man in for refreshments.

'*Nein*,' said the young man sullenly, refusing to meet anyone's eyes.

Finally, he was persuaded to come in but he began a brusque conversation with Grass in which he seemed to be suggesting that Grass was a communist. Finally, Grass turned to me and asked me if I could speak French. I said I could and we all repaired into his sixteenth-century farmhouse, leaving the young man to sulk outside.

Grass was charming, a gentle and kindly man, sensitive and artistic. We spoke for a while and when the work was out of the way, he asked us where we planned on having dinner.

'Back at Hamburg,' said Dom.

'Hamburg is like a student's hostel. It will be closed by the time you reach,' said Grass. He directed our guide to a local ratskeller where we could have a meal.

The three of us did go there. Across the room sat a German family, pink and white and truculent. The woman in particular kept glaring at Dom. She called the owner over to her table a couple of times and lectured him, pointing at Dom.

Finally, I could stand it no longer.

I called the owner over and told him to tell the Frau that if she pointed again, I would be very glad to pour a jug of water over her head. We were two Asians in a Caucasian world and the sense I got was that she wanted us out of there as quickly as possible so that she could go back to her pink-and-white world. Mein host was very embarrassed but he was helpless to deny one of his best customers—the Frau and her family were rather porcine—and he could not offend us either.

'Now, I have a real treat for you,' said the young man and drove us through the dark evening to a big barn that was brightly lit. Inside, there were hundreds of young men and women. At the door, a young man, blonde and blue-eyed and Nordic, gave our guide a stiff-armed salute. I began to suspect the worst as we walked into a world full of the dream children of Adolf. We were seated at trestle tables while our guide climbed on to the stage and sang *Uber Alles* and some mountain songs.

The leader came over, a middle-aged man with a scar down one cheek.

'Are you enjoying yourselves with my children?' he asked.

'You have many children,' I said.

'Thousands,' he said, 'thousands. We climb mountains and we grow strong. We will come back and make Germany our own again.'

Suddenly our guide's refusal to have anything to do with Grass began to make sense. Grass was seen then as a communist. He was seen as someone who had stood against the Third Reich. While this vastly enhanced his status as a writer in the international community, it didn't do much for his position among the neo-Nazis who wanted to wear jackboots and hate people for an accident of birth.

I told Dom that I couldn't bear it and wanted to leave. He agreed and we made our departure hastily.

The newspapers tell me that Grass has admitted that as a very young man he was part of the Nazis. I cannot reconcile the gentle man we met with the jackbooted boys swilling their beer in that hall.

SIXTEEN

Leela Naidu, Editor

Ramnath Goenka had been Frank Moraes's last boss and perhaps he felt that he owed Dom something. Over a Marwari thali, he gave us our marching orders.

'You,' he told Dom 'will be the editor of the *Sunday Standard*.'

So that was Dom put in charge of the Sunday edition of the *Indian Express*.

'And you,' he turned to me, 'will be my communications manager.'

I must have looked a little surprised. I had not applied for the job. Neither of us had discussed a job for me with the old man. But when you are confronted with an autocrat at the dining table, you have very little choice.

'I have no experience of that kind of thing,' I said.

'I have these Marwaris who sell my newspaper as if they were still in the cloth markets of Calcutta,' he snarled. 'You will be better than them, at any rate. You can't be much worse.'

So that was how Dom Moraes and Leela Naidu ended up working for Ramnath Goenka in the one thousand nine hundred and eighty-first year of Our Lord.

Oddly enough, my first job as a communications manager had to do with designing the empty first floor of his Express Towers at Nariman Point, Mumbai. It was a rather wonderful space, since it opened out on to a grass bed that had been placed on the terrace around it. The building had been designed by Joseph Allen Stein, the man who came to India in the 1950s and made it his home, building the Triveni Kala Sangam arts complex, the India International Centre and many other prestigious structures. I suspect that Margaret, his wife, an architectural botanist (!) might have had a hand in the decision about the grass bed.

There was a whole lot of unused furniture in the godowns of the old Express buildings and I excavated the lot. There were some really elegant trestle tables, spare and simple. I brought those in and teamed them with some chairs which had wrought-iron legs. I thought it all worked together quite well with the cork screens lined with khadi that I used to partition the huge space. I felt that the screens would create some divisions, but also retain the transparency and democracy that I thought were part of a press office. But then the chairs that were placed around the conference table began to vanish. Everyone wanted four chairs in their cubicles and each morning I had to send scouts out to bring the chairs back to the conference table. In order to stop the chair-poaching, I asked for *mora*s (Indian cane stools) so that everyone got a couple of chairs and a couple of moras.

That was easy. What was difficult was the hostility of the old guard who resented me immediately. I understood what they must have been feeling. They probably saw me as a society lady who had been foisted on them because she had once been an actress and her husband was a poet. I tried to involve them but they refused to cooperate. The only support I had was from L.K. Jha who as our business correspondent, perhaps, understood the importance of advertising and would tell me what stories he had planned so that we could drum up a little support around them.

'You can't pull these people along. You can't push them along,' Goenka said impatiently when I talked to him. 'Just go on and do what you want.'

That was easy for him to say, but it got difficult to do a one-person job when I could see a whole bunch of people who were supposed to help me, sitting back and smoking cigarettes and trying to make sure I failed. By this time, my mother was also ill and that meant I had two parents who needed looking after. It was during this period too that my mother was hospitalised. She had to undergo two operations for the cancer of the lymph nodes. She was being treated by Dr Praful Desai, head of the Tata Memorial Hospital. I spent each night with her at the hospital. At six in the morning, the nurse would come for a blood sample. When it had been drawn, I would follow her to the duty station and see that it was labelled properly.

'They mean well, Leela,' said my father, 'but they might mix up the vials or mislabel them. Any false results at this time could be dangerous.'

I would make sure my mother had her breakfast and then cross town to Nariman Point to work at the *Express*. Then I would come home to make lunch for Daddy and then go back to work. After that, I would come home to give Daddy his dinner and go to Tata Memorial for night duty. It was gruelling and I didn't even have time to notice whether Dom was having problems or getting on well at the *Express*. But then I suspect it was the former for by the beginning of the following year, Dom had resigned.

'Go, go,' said Goenka to him. 'I'm keeping Leela.'

'She won't stay if I go,' said Dom.

We were already in a state of rapid decline so after a little thought I decided it would be best to resign too. When I resigned too, everything went back to its normal pace.

Not even a month had gone by when Nari Hira, who had turned his company, Magna Publishing, into something of a byword with *Stardust* and *Society*, turned up in a three-piece suit. It was March and he did seem a little over-dressed for a man who had just recovered from a cardiac operation. Sipping his iced water, he told me that he was looking for an editor for *Society*.

'Isn't Shobha De the editor?' I asked.

'She has resigned.'

'And her second-in-command?'

'He turned the job down.'

Oddly enough, Shobha herself had featured me on the first cover of *Society*. Nari Hira had read the story and decided that I was the person who could replace her. I have no idea what had made him think so but he refused to explain any further.

'I am not a regular reader of *Society*,' I warned him.

'Which is why I want you to edit it. I want you to create the kind of magazine you would read,' he said.

'I'm not really interested in society ladies and parties,' I added. I thought this might frighten him but he said I could remake the magazine in the shape I wanted. This was carte blanche editorial control and I thought I should enjoy it.

And so I made a list of articles we should do and people who should be interviewed. When I arrived at the office, I was escorted to Shobha's cabin and peacock chair. This, I took to be a piece of irony, either on Shobha's part or on the part of whoever had designed it. I surveyed my new domain and found that three hostile pairs of eyes were fixed upon me. But I had a job to do and I assumed that journalists would not have the same pettiness as mid-level marketing managers so I explained what I thought *Society* should be like.

I explained that in my view of it society did not mean only high society. We should feature a cobbler just so long as the cobbler had an interesting story to tell. And then I shared my list of ideas with them.

They all declared that they loved the ideas, but it was going to be difficult to accommodate them since they had locked in all the stories for the next two issues.

'Well,' I said, determined to look on the positive side, 'I suppose we can all work on this list in the meanwhile.'

They looked a bit green, but it was difficult for them to be too obstreperous all at once.

I thought about things for a while and then went to see Mr Hira with my list. He noticed that I had J.R.D. Tata, the charismatic industrialist and aviator, on my list of people to be interviewed.

'Do you know J.R.D.?' he asked.

I did, of course. His wife, Thelly, was a good friend and he had been my Uncle Jeh for a long time.

'Have you been to his house?'

I had, of course.

'Then if he agrees to an interview, we'll put him on the next cover.'

'I don't think that will be possible,' I said, all innocent and dewy-eyed.

'Why not?' he asked.

'You see, my staff says that the next two issues are locked in.'

'I think you will find that some pages will have suddenly become vacant,' he smiled, in saturnine fashion.

And so it was agreed that I should interview J.R.D. Tata, who had not been interviewed since *Life* magazine had in its heyday, done a profile on him. We went to his house and shot him with the children he had 'adopted'. These were the children of his staff, whom he was educating. The cover picture, which was taken on the lawn of his home, had him surrounded by these children. It was quite a different story from the business boilerplate that had been published about him.

Another story idea that caused some more pages to be unlocked was an interview with Dr Praful Desai who was the director of Tata Memorial Hospital and the chief surgeon there as well. He had treated my mother for cancer and called her his platinum brick because she never complained through two major operations and chemotherapy as well. We did a long interview in which he spoke movingly about the shortage of medicines, the shortage of doctors and of the way he had often thought of euthanasia for his terminally ill patients who were kept alive artificially.

As soon as Nari Hira went off to his nest in New York, the old guard began to wail. Their resistance took the form of noncooperation. I'd suggest an idea and either the staff would tell me it had been done before or it wasn't interesting or someone would agree to do it and then produce excuse after excuse for not doing it. They rather liked their society ladies and the sickly scent of too much perfume. So I did the only thing a fella could do; I left. I did not even pick up my last salary.

The next time I became editor was in 1982. Darryl D'Monte, a journalist and Dom's cousin, told me that a certain Alok Mandelia had asked him to create a monthly features magazine. There was no other brief but Mandelia had a name for it. It would be called *Keynote*. Darryl suggested my name and I was hired as managing editor. I hired the poet Manohar Shetty as the editor.

Mr Mandelia was a bit surprised.

'You're mad. He's running a restaurant and he comes to the office for only two hours a day. How is he going to edit?'

'He will do his work,' I said, although I was getting varicose veins in my eyes from proofreading copy.

David Davidar was one of the young men who came to pay homage to Dom. When he heard that I was managing editor of *Keynote*, he announced that he would leave his job with the *Christian Science Monitor* and work with us as literary editor.

Mandelia was often indisposed which was why I had a free hand. He would sometimes object to the seriousness of the magazine but I would point at our circulation figures which seemed to be rising. This irked him. He would have preferred, I often thought, to have the magazine fail so he could prove that people really did want to read gossip. But when there was nothing else, he would ask why I did not write an editorial.

'Because I think of the whole magazine as one editorial,' I said.

He seemed rather dumbfounded by that. When I did introduce a note to the reader, he didn't like that either.

'What do you mean by this line, "We hope you will be difficult to please. Please send in your views to us"?' he asked.

I didn't know how to explain that one, but fortunately he was off on another of his hobby-horses and I listened with only half an ear.

A friend of mine asked me recently, after looking through some of the old issues, how we had managed to be so left-of-centre.

'If carrying articles on children working in dangerous situations, and how retirement benefits are rarely enough to allow the old to live with dignity is left-of-centre, then I suppose we were,' I replied.

But in reality, I think, the ideological biases were an accident of the time and the people involved. It was not as if we sought to position ourselves in a particular space. We ended up there because we shared the same kind of values and because the intelligent in those days did seem to be on the pinker side of the spectrum. But if we carried articles about India's tribals or the marginalisation of the poor in cities or even the atrophy of Sanskrit, it was because no one else seemed to be doing it at the time.

Ruskin Bond heard about the magazine, read it and wrote to me, saying that he would like to contribute. I had always enjoyed his gentle prose and his effortless style and so I sent him a welcoming letter. (This was in the days before email, and when telephones did not fit into the back-pocket of your jeans. And Ruskin, always a bit of a Luddite, didn't have a telephone anyway.) Adil Jussawalla, the poet, was a regular columnist too. His column was always on time, always funny and never entirely comprehensible.

We were at work on the seventh issue, already putting it to bed, when we discovered that the printers, Mandelia's distant relatives, had not been paid, not even for the first issue. When Mandelia found out we knew, he locked us out. Then David, tall and short-tempered, rang me up one morning. His message was crisp, 'Don't come to the office. I've broken down the door.'

He cleared the office of his books and then came over to chat. He didn't think to clear mine as well or else I might not have lost several books to which I was sentimentally attached.

And so *Keynote* folded. The staff would visit me every day for the next months or so—hanging on to the hope that Mad Mandy might pay his bills, the doors might open and the magazine be started again. But as time went by, they all went on to other jobs.

SEVENTEEN

'Have You Stopped Acting?'

I cannot remember how many times I have been asked, 'Have you stopped acting?'

I have never worked out a good enough reply. I wanted something witty like that famous exchange in *Sunset Boulevard* where William Holden as Joe Gillis says, 'You're Norma Desmond. You used to be in silent pictures. You used to be big.' Swanson, as Norma Desmond retorts, without missing a beat, 'I *am* big. It's the pictures that got small.'

But does an actor stop acting? Or do they stop getting roles? Had I stopped getting roles? And how could anyone ask that? Perhaps they were being polite, but it always seemed like a somewhat dangerous question so I always gave a tame answer.

But then, I don't blame the film industry. Directors would have to see me around to cast me. Cinema works on the principle of 'Out of sight, out of mind'. Dom and I left India for Hong Kong in 1971 and we returned to Mumbai a decade later.

But one evening at Habiba and Mario Miranda's Colaba home, I found myself sitting next to Shyam Benegal, who asked me if I had stopped acting. I had seen some of his films and thought he was an interesting director. I had also featured in two of his commercials.

I told him that I had not turned my back on acting.

He said, 'I have a role for you.'

I raised an eyebrow, only because I did not know whether he had discovered the role there and then or he had thought about it earlier and was suggesting it because we had met by serendipity at a friend's house.

'I know you will want to read the script and you will only take it if you like it,' he said. My reputation was alive and well, I could see.

Much later, I heard the inside story. The role was supposed to be played by Madhur Jaffrey. Negotiations had broken down over the pounds and the pence. Like almost every film I have been involved in, this one too was a low-budget one and there were no pounds for Madhur, only pence. I was paid something that looked like an honorarium for the three months that I was on the sets. I wish some day someone would ring me up to say, 'We have a huge budget and we would love to pay you a huge amount of money so name your price.' Of course, that would probably be the kind of film that I wouldn't want to do anyway, but it is nice to think of it happening.

A few days later, Nira Benegal called up to say that she was going to send me the scene synopses. I had rather hoped for a script, but of course, that wasn't ready. As in all the other films I had worked on, it would be served to the actors, piping hot, every morning, by Shama Zaidi who wrote many of Shyam's films. But the scene synopses did at least allow me to see how the character of Dona Maria Souza-Soares developed. I liked what I read, the odd mix between the history of the times and the magical realism that Shyam enjoyed so much. Besides—or should the word be beneath?—this story was both a subaltern narrative of family and a grand narrative involving Kushtoba, the Robin Hood-like figure who had defied the Portuguese colonisers of Goa and the family that had given him up to the Portuguese: the Miranda family in whose home we were shooting.

Trikaal (Past, Present, Future) was written in *chust* Urdu. Of course, there is a little coda in the beginning of the film where Naseeruddin Shah as Ruiz Pereira, the narrator who now lives in the modern world of Bombay, says that it would be easier for the audience to understand if everyone in the film spoke Hindi instead of Portuguese but I was not convinced by that. I didn't think many people were. It's a part of the whole pretence of cinema that people speak a language we understand. But that was probably another experiment in pointing up the difference between reality and spectacle. I didn't mind the Urdu; I have always liked to have my lines in Devanagri because it helps me immerse myself in the script, in the culture. Only here, I was immersing myself in a Lusitanian–Indian hybrid culture—best illustrated in the moment in which Dona Maria refuses a co-religionist as a match for her daughter on caste grounds—while reading chaste Urdu written in Devanagri.

At one point, an assistant director came to me with my lines. It might have been Aditya Bhattacharya, the grandson of Bimal Roy and a nice young man. I began reading a long line that I had to say. It had to do with the notion of Time as a plank placed over a well. The plank, in this metaphor, does not reach the other side of the well and yet we were all walking on it. In my head, I began to visualise the words to be able to get a better hold of what they meant. But it soon became clear that if one tried to walk on planks balanced on one side of a well, one would soon fall in. Perhaps it was something deeper but I did not quite understand. So I went to Shyam and asked him if he could explain it to me. He dug his spectacles out of his pocket and surveyed the lines.

'I'm not sure what they mean either,' he said for he was and is an honest man. Then he looked at me quizzically and smiled.

The assistant director came back about half an hour later and told me that the shoot had been cancelled since the dialogue wasn't ready. Shama continued to be perfectly civil to me but I couldn't help feeling that there was something a little, how shall I say this, a little acidic about her smile.

The set was well-stocked with women. There was Shama who seemed to have a proprietary interest in Shyam. There was Neena Gupta who had a problem playing my maid; she felt that it was not a role suited to her dignity and her knowledge of Sanskrit. There was Ila Arun, with whom Neena Gupta would gossip. And there was poor Sushma Prakash who was a newcomer and seemed bewildered by all this sorority.

Before shooting could start, Saba Zaidi, who was related to Shama in some way, came to visit me. She was the costume designer of the film and wanted to look at 'my French clothes'. I could see the point of that. This was a rich Portuguese family that we were playing and it would never do for them to be dressed in the tacky maxis that costume designers think screen Catholics wear. The Souza-Soareses would have been the comprador class and they would have been up to every fashion trick Paris could dish out, if they were to be invited to the houses of their colonial overlords.

When she left, I was sitting in a welter of tissue paper and had promised to carry a good many of the sartorial relics of my youth with me. They were all in perfect condition because they were exquisite clothes, made by people who cared about perfection and because my mother had put them away with love.

My mother was a woman who liked her hats so I took some of them including four metres of black Chantilly lace that she had bought many years earlier in Paris. This was cut up to make my widow's weeds. There was my Lanvin Castillo, a pink hand-stitched *dentelle*, iridescent with sequins which Sushma wore. The lace was made by Marescot, one of the greatest lace-makers of France. I had a moiré silk by Dior with flowers delicately woven into it, which Anita Kanwar wore. Sabira Merchant wore my yellow Chanel suit with its amber-coloured buttons. I took bags and gloves too but the way they were treated made me swear never to try and help again. Claire Booth Luce once said that no good deed ever goes unpunished and when Anita Kanwar stepped backwards like a great galoot and tore the hem; when I found the Lanvin on the floor of the dressing room, when the whole lot were returned to me without the benefit of dry-cleaning, when I was not even given a token hiring charge, I decided that Clare knew what she was talking about. To add a final delicate touch of irony, Saba Zaidi got the National Award for Costume Design.

In addition, Shyam wanted me to lose weight as we went along so that my clothes should hang upon my frame. I have never been overweight, but he was the director. So I began a diet that I knew would help me lose weight steadily and healthily. There's no secret to it. It involves eating less, no meat, no wheat, no sweet. Just grilled fish and lots of salads, which you wash yourself in pinky water. For those who do not know what pinky water is, it's the name for a solution of potassium permanganate which oxidises the germs. The diet worked.

But in the end, when I watched it, I was glad I did the film. Shyam seemed at ease in the milieu, one of ease and privilege. I found the film itself a little diffused in that Shyam seemed to have many ideas and he wanted to put all of them in at once. Some of them, I thought, didn't go anywhere but many of my upper-caste Goan Catholic friends have said that it rang several bells in their heads. There was no electricity in Loutolim, where we were shooting, and so the director of photography, Ashok Mehta, the perfectionist who slaved over each shot despite a bleeding ulcer, had to make do with natural light and candlelight and no doubt the reflection of all those lights in the sweat on our faces.

EIGHTEEN

The British on a Hunger Strike in the Land of the Mahatma

Five thirty in the morning in Pachmarhi, a small hill station in Madhya Pradesh, shooting for *Electric Moon*. I wake up and I am as cold as when I went to bed the night before. I wonder whether I am getting that old. My bones creak as I get out of bed. Even a bucket of boiling water for my bath leaves no dent in the cold in my bones. The air outside was beyond crisp, beyond cold. Central India is always cold during the winter and up in the hills it is cooler but in 1990–91, it was a genuine bona fide cold spell that had even sent cool fingers down Mumbai's over-heated spine. We often awoke to frozen pipes in the cars that were ferrying us around the small town that had once been the summer capital of the Central Provinces. Shivering, I made my way to the green room where I would find my costume, beautiful mulmul kaftans designed by the art director, Arundhati Roy, and open Kolhapuri slippers, which were later to give me hypothermia.

'The show must go on,' I would mumble to myself as my teeth chattered with the cold. 'The show must go on and I am going to turn into an icicle.' On my way from the green room, clad inadequately but elegantly, I glanced out and beheld a red elephant.

An imp of mischief, never too far from the surface, made me

knock on producer Bobby Bedi's office door. 'Rani,' I told him, when he opened the door, 'is red.'

That international tribe that is known as 'film people', see the world through the lens of their own involvement in it. A flower is not a flower; it is of questionable value if it is to be used in a scene. Who can be sure it will look as fresh tomorrow, if the scene has to be re-shot? Who can be sure another flower will be found that will be a proper match? And a flowering branch of a tree, often used to establish perspective, can drive the continuity persons to distraction and they in turn can drive the director of photography round the bend. A change in the sun will change its shadow. And there is always the possibility that the arrangement of leaves, today such a perfect pattern of light and shade, can suddenly vanish.

Old film wisdom has it that shooting with children and animals is always difficult so Bobby must have been ready for some trouble from the elephants in the cast. But among the many things that animals do *not* do to make life difficult for producers is changing colour.

Bobby Bedi, the continuity person and I went out to my friend Rani, a one-and-a-half-year-old pachyderm with perfect manners. She was one of two elephants—the other, a male, was called predictably enough, Raja—on loan to us from Gemini Studios. Whenever she saw me, she would amble over and carefully lift up the flap of the pocket on my safari shirt, if I was wearing one, or send her trunk investigating discreetly down from the side of my blouse. She was looking for the wild guavas I would pluck for her in the evening when the shoot was over.

One day, when I was sitting under the shamiana in the middle of a shot, the director of photography called a halt. 'Leela,' he said quietly, 'Look behind you.'

I turned and there was Rani. She had sneaked up behind me and her trunk had eased its way around under the pink georgette of my sari and around my tummy. All this so delicately that I hadn't felt a thing.

That morning Rani looked a little sheepish, if it is possible for several tonnes of elephant to look sheepish. On her way to the shoot, she had obviously stopped at a fallow field and given herself a mud bath. The red was only temporary and would wash off.

Electric Moon was about the royalty of India, after the lapse of the privy purses. Gerson da Cunha played a former maharaja called Bubbles and I played Sukanya or Socks, his sister. Our third sibling Ranveer, played by Roshan Seth, has the charm and the drive that it takes to build a tourist industry out of an illusion. I think the film was supposed to be a comedy. I think it was supposed to be a critique of a certain kind of cultural colonialism, a counterpoint to the British Raj, but I can't be sure.

I suppose I could have asked Pradip Kishen. He was supposed to be the director but it was quite clear to me, at least, who was in charge. So I asked Arundhati Roy about a scene. 'Think about dosas,' she said.

I didn't ask for much help with direction after that. I tried to think my way into Sukanya's character for myself. I was determined to play her straight because I had been told that the film was a comedy. According to me, the best way to play a comic character is to forget that it is a comic character. The funniest people are those who are doing stupid things in an extremely serious way. But Arundhati was having none of that. She got into it with Simon Tytherleigh, the make-up man on the set.

'She looks too glamorous,' she complained. 'Make her lips into a square.'

He refused to do any such thing. I tried to stay out of it. Finally, after they had been at it for a while, he said, 'I can paint her lips right up to her nostrils and she will still look the same.'

Ms Roy retired defeated and Simon and I shared a conspiratorial wink.

I must say I admire the way that Arundhati Roy has turned her status as celebrity author into a catalyst for the causes she cares about, but there was very little of the caring Ms Roy on the set of

Electric Moon. One of the first shots was supposed to be a spoof of the dance sequences of Indian cinema from *Chandralekha* to *Jhanak Jhanak Paayal Baaje*. As Socks, I was seated under a shamiana with the Tamil producer and supposed to be making conversation. Easy enough for us, but the dancers were having a tough time of it since they were out in the open, under the sun. No lunch had been organised for them, there was no place where they could rest in the shade in between shots, and the pace was gruelling. Finally, Giles Nuttgens, the director of photography, signalled that it was time to pack up because the sunlight was fading. The lead dancer and I walked back to the hunting lodge where I was staying and I could see that she was stumbling with fatigue. I put my arm around her to steady her because the winding path ran next to a steep drop hundreds of feet down, when a familiar voice spoke.

'Why are you doing that, Leela?' asked Arundhati, 'She's supposed to be a dancer. She should have some sense of balance.'

The girl gulped.

'She terrifies me,' she whispered.

One of the strangest things that happened on the set was the affair of the china plates. The meals were a mess, swimming in oil and oddly mixed spices. But to make matters worse, we were served in plates made of sal leaves, stitched together with pieces of stick or thorn. The china plates, with their fussy decorative designs, were used for the gardeners, carpenters and cleaners and the like, whom Arundhati depended on.

On the first day, everyone noticed but not a word was said. The British tried to pretend that this was part of the Great Indian Experience, even as thick red oil slipped from between the cracks in the leaves and dropped between their legs. The maalis and the cleaners ate awkwardly, as if afraid their nails might hurt the designs on the plates. Or at least, when we saw them eating since they were served first. As the poor and the disenfranchised will do, they would heap their plates and leave very little for the cast and the crew. This was rather amusing for a day or two but in a few days, the rumblings—some of which came from British bellies unaccustomed to oil and spice in such degrees—grew into a storm. Then Giles Nuttgens decided that he had had enough. One day, he walked up to the buffet and surveyed the remains of the feast. Then he put down his sal leaf plate and announced that he was not going to eat. The rest of the cast followed suit, gratefully. The humour of this situation struck me: the British on a hunger strike in the land of the Mahatma? Somewhere the jug-eared man I had met once with a bunch of gladioli and some fine chocolates must be laughing.

Bobby Bedi was not amused.

'Can't we have some mince?' asked one crew member.

'Has no one in India heard of a salad?' asked another.

'Let me into that kitchen and I'll cook myself a boiled egg,' said a third.

Bobby looked like he might even have allowed that had he not seen me wiggling my eyebrows frantically. I had visited the kitchen and had watched as cockroaches wandered around in the manner of much-loved domestic animals. And so it fell to my lot to visit the market and buy some fresh vegetables. I couldn't understand why we weren't getting some delightful greens, since we were suffering from the cold that these veggies love. It could only be that the khansama didn't know or didn't care.

On the way to the market, I noticed an agricultural institute set in the middle of some stunted trees that looked like . . . olive trees? Indeed, they were olive trees and there on the windswept plain of Pachmarhi, they were slowly dying of frost-bite. But the gardeners could be suborned and so I got myself some baby cabbage and romaine lettuce from the vegetable gardens of the institute. Then we took a large unused flower bed and turned it into a kitchen garden. From then on we could have salads.

After we had managed to get rid of some of the cockroaches, I taught the khansama how to make an ersatz mince stew with local herbs. But the salad was a bigger battle. First, I had to teach the man how to make a solution of pinky water so as to rid the veggies of the germs. Next, I had to teach him not to wash the vegetables in water from the tap again. Then, I had to establish the principles of a basic vinaigrette.

'Nimbu aur tel?' he asked, his brow furrowing over the idea of lime and oil. 'Nimbu aur tel?'

'Nimbu aur tel,' I said.

On another occasion, we had a fire. One of the big klieg lights caught fire over my head. The crew rushed me out but the electrician, a young man, had eyes only for his precious equipment. In his mad dash to save it, he gashed his hand on some rusty barbed wire. The British crew and I rushed to him with their first aid boxes but it was a deep slash. The only thing we could do was to pull the edges together and seal it with black masking tape. (Sounds horrible? It works as a temporary measure.) We sent him off to get stitched up properly—of course, there was no doctor on the set—and then went off for a break. After this whole tamasha, we found Arundhati weeping on Pradip's shoulder. But she wasn't concerned about the electrician. She was worried about her stuffed animals.

And so when I watch her pleading for the disenfranchised and the marginalised, I think back to the ruthless Ms Roy on that sun-drenched plateau in Madhya Pradesh and I wonder whether it is easier for us to sympathise with anonymous masses than with the actual people we are confronted with in real life. The poor are an abstraction for whom we can all feel an ambiguous benevolence. The smelly, sticky, importunate person in front of us? Now that can be a different matter altogether.

Perhaps I am misjudging all of them, but I often feel that a production house can be judged by the way it treats those who have no voice: the extras, the dancers and the animals. One day, Rani seemed to be a little quiet. I saw a tear run down her cheek. I asked the mahout what the matter was.

'Rani is hungry,' he told me.

The arrangements that had been made for the elephants were

extremely rudimentary. So I stopped work and said that I would only start again when they had been fed. I suppose one might say that it was unprofessional but it has always been my way of protesting. Finally, I had to send one of the spot boys off to the town myself to get huge bunches of bananas, and two huge jerry cans so that they could be watered regularly.

'And jaggery please, Madam,' said the mahout.

'Jaggery?'

'It is good for sunstroke.'

Elephants, I later discovered, have no sweat glands and therefore can suffer from sunstroke if they have to stand around in the sun for hours as Raja and Rani were made to do. The elephants munched their way through the bananas and the jaggery and we all went back to work.

The day before they were to leave, the mahout came up to me and said, 'Rani would like to take you for a ride.'

I climbed on to her knee and then perched myself on her head, behind her ears and we set off into the forests of the Sahyadris. If you have ever ridden an elephant through the jungle, you'll know this was a very special experience. Once you've aligned your spine and let the rhythm into your body, it is the perfect way to experience a forest. Rani had perfect manners; I never had to even duck my head as we walked through the green and gold of a forest morning. An hour later, we were back and a day later, we bid each other a sniffly goodbye.

~

I don't think terribly many people 'got' *Electric Moon*. It was the opening feature film at the Bangalore Festival of Films in 1992–93. We had a press conference and a gimlet-eyed lady stood up and asked me, 'What is the meaning of this incestuous relationship you have with your brother in the film?'

I almost goggled at her. But I recovered enough to say, 'Madam, it was very virginal.'

NINETEEN

Season of Mists and Mellow Fruitfulness

'You must be ready for this kind of thing now that you are in the autumn of your life,' said the young doctor. I gritted my teeth against the pain in my hip and decided to ignore him and his clichés. Autumn of life? I was born in 1940. Anyone who wants may calculate my age. Then if they want to call me old, they have my permission. But 'autumn of life'? That was adding insult to the injury I had done myself by falling and breaking my hip socket and femur.

But later that evening, as I read Keats in bed, I rediscovered the 'Ode to Autumn':

Season of mists and mellow fruitfulness!
Close bosom-friend of the maturing sun;
Conspiring with him how to load and bless
With fruit the vines that round the thatch-eaves run;
To bend with apples the mossed cottage-trees,
And fill all fruit with ripeness to the core . . .

After I had managed to turn myself into a cliché—women my age are supposed to fall; it's practically de rigueur—I was taken to St. Elizabeth's Nursing Home. The doctors came and chirruped bluffly at me and I was wheeled into the operation theatre and wheeled out again with five hundred and fifty grams of metal holding my right leg together.

'Do you remember me?'

I had begun to recover and here was a young woman. Her face was vaguely familiar but nothing came back.

'I was your student.'

French? No.

'At Bal Anand.'

That was a very long time ago, but in the same country at any rate. No, in the same area. St. Elizabeth's is not far from the home of Nandini Mehta, sister of Pupul Jaykar, both of whom were close to Jiddu Krishnamurti, who has been described as one of the greatest philosophers of the twentieth century. (To me he was also one of the old souls whom I met, someone who was obviously enlightened.)

When I filed a suit for custody of my twins and lost, Pupul Jaykar called me and in her gruff but caring fashion, gave me my marching orders. I was to go and see Krishnamurti, she said. At that point, I simply took down the address, noted the time and made my way there.

'Ah,' said Krishnamurti, when we met, 'The mother.'

I was a little startled by this.

'I saw you and your daughters in the gardens of the Oberoi in Srinagar,' he said. 'You were on your hands and knees with the children.'

I remembered.

I had given both my daughters magnifying glasses and we were exploring in the garden, discovering 'a world in a grain of sand, And Heaven in a wild flower', as Blake puts it in that glorious poem, *Auguries of Innocence*.

Priya announced that she wanted to go to the bathroom. As the twins were toddlers, I thought it would do no one any harm if she were to go out in the open.

'Just find a place where no one can see you,' I said.

So Priya went up to a Chinar tree and lowered away. By her childish logic, if she could not see anyone, no one could see her.

Krishnaji handed me a tissue. It was only then that I realised I was crying. I wept on and on, quietly.

'Let it all come out,' he said. But his kindness was veined with a total honesty. 'You will always see your children through a glass wall,' he said.

It was not the remark an ordinary person might make to a woman who has just had her most precious ones taken away from her. But then Krishnaji was no ordinary person. He was compassionate but he was also relentless. He was preparing me for what he saw and he would offer me no false hopes. He was not going to pat me on the head and say that it would be all right.

I cried for a long time.

When I returned home, I told my father, half-teasing, half-serious, 'I've found myself a grandfather.'

We met regularly after that, Krishnaji and I, whenever we were in the same city. Dom was rather dismissive of what he called 'Leela's godman' but I finally managed to introduce the two of them at the Hotel Pierre in New York.

There was a bit of a twinkle in Krishnaji's eye. 'Frank used to tell me that he was allergic to all gurus,' he said. 'I suspect you are too.'

Dom was disarmed and they got along well after that. When we were working on *Voices for Life*, I suggested his name as one of the people who might contribute. Krishnaji agreed to be interviewed but asked for the money that the UNFPA would pay to be donated to his school at Ojai in California.

I took Heff, Dom's son, to see him once.

'Leela says you can cure anything,' said Heff, peering up into that aquiline face with the impertinence of childhood. 'My nose bleeds.'

Krishnaji laid his hands on Heff and that was the end of the nose bleeds. But it wasn't that which drew me to him. He had the rare ability to give you his full attention and the even more rare ability to generate a genuine companionable silence. I met him once in England, where I had gone with a friend who was undergoing treatment at Osterley Park. He was staying with friends in Wimbledon so I went there to meet him. I found him watching a documentary on the slaughter of baby seals. He seemed deeply moved.

We went for a walk in a park, full of nannies and their charges. After a while, we sat down together, each of us silent, watching the children play. I could see a toddler heading towards a fountain. The sunlight was refracting through the spray and the little one was delighted. She wanted a rainbow and she was going to get one. Fat fingers outstretched, she began to climb the edge of the fountain.

I was on my feet and running even before I knew it.

I reached her just as she discovered the truth about rainbows and the temperature of water in Wimbledon in the month of June. I picked her out, wet and outraged at her dunking, but none the worse for that.

Her nanny turned up, moments later, horrified at how quickly her charge had taken advantage of a few minutes of inattention. I restored the child and advised a change of clothes, a hot drink and a nap and returned to Krishnaji.

'You really want to be a mother,' he said and he said it with that extraordinary mixture of compassion and understanding that was his alone.

The last time I met him, I was forty-one. My mother had died that year, after battling cancer for a year. I dressed her in one of her favourite dresses and put a few lilies in her hands, which was all the crematorium would allow. Then I escorted her body to Chandanwadi. Perhaps it has something to do with the fact that they deal with death so much. Perhaps it has something to do with the low pay and bad work conditions. As her body vanished behind a leather curtain, one of the ghouls beckoned to me. I looked in his direction and for some reason that I have never been able to fathom, he raised the curtain to let me see my mother's slim feet enveloped in flames. I was over four months pregnant and felt as if someone had twisted a dagger in my belly.

I came home and a few days later began spotting. Later that night, I miscarried. It was a baby boy. He had long toes, like Dom.

'Do you want a shoe box?' I was asked.

A shoe box?

'To take your baby home in,' said the nurse.

My mother had seven miscarriages. Seven boys died. I was the only survivor. At this low point, I thought about her and about her last miscarriage.

~

October, 1946. Mumbai was very hot and perhaps to get my mother away from the muggy heat of the city, Daddy organised a trip to Lahore where Sarojini Naidu's sister was the principal of Gangaram College. After that we were supposed to go on to Kashmir. For the first half of the journey, we travelled by train, in a coupé, a bed-sit on wheels. From Lahore, we travelled by car. Daddy had organised two majors from the British army to escort us. From Rawalpindi, landslides had made the road rough and bumpy. Mummy was heavy with child. Although she was feeling ill, she never said a word. By the time we reached Srinagar, she was bleeding.

'Excuse me,' I said, 'My mother is bleeding.'

The two majors, who had cleared the road, were horrified. They rushed us to our hotel and called the best doctor they could find but she miscarried again.

'Little one,' said the doctor, 'you should not be in the room.'

I was told to sit on a bench at the end of the corridor. The doctor came out with something small in his arms, pathetically small.

'Close your eyes,' he told me.

I closed them and the scent of the pine floor filled my nostrils. A lovely clean scent which was soon mixed with the smell of iron, a smell I did not like instinctively.

My mother was weak, lying in the bed, her translucent skin even paler.

'A storm is brewing,' she said.

I knew that that meant the wild mushrooms would be out. So I went to the kitchen and got myself a wicker basket. I spent that evening looking for mushrooms under the stones on the lawn. I wanted her to have the mushroom omelettes that she loved. I would take them to her and she would tell me which were poisonous and which were not. She had learnt about mushrooms from her father.

Each evening, the chowkidar (watchman) watched as I went looking for Mummy's mushrooms. After a week he gave me a little jumper with red pompoms on it, a jumper he had knitted for me through the long quiet watches of the night.

My mother was touched and wanted to give him a gift.

'Not at all,' he refused, 'I knit for all my children. My wife can't knit.'

If there is a lesson in that, it concerns the incidental kindness of strangers.

By the second day, my mother must have been tired of mushrooms and mushroom omelettes. But she bore with me and ate them with every expression of delight. She must have known it was my way of trying to do something for her. She allowed it because she knew I had to heal too.

~

I thought of her as I contemplated the offer of a shoe box.

I did not know what to say. I did not know if I could go to the crematorium again. Dom was in Madhya Pradesh, where he was working on *Answered by Flutes*, though he would fly home the next day.

'What will you do with him otherwise?'

'We throw them away with the used bandages,' she said.

Dom whisked me off to Bhopal to cheer me up. Flying was not a good idea. One of my legs swelled up until it was twice the size of the other. Then Daddy began to have his mini-strokes. He began to get weaker and weaker and complained of memory loss. But he still played chess with his customary brilliance and when young scientists came to visit him, they marvelled at the lucidity of his thought processes. I could see how much he loved those visits. His eyes lit up when he was surrounded by brash young men, all trying to impress the legendary Dr Ramaiah Naidu.

At forty-one, this can be a heavy burden to bear and when I met Krishnaji again, in the middle of a perfectly ordinary conversation, I burst into tears.

He did not stop me from crying but he did ask politely, after I had blown my nose, why I was crying.

'I don't know,' I said. 'I carry this pool of grief within me always. I suppose I'm crying for the world. The wars. The children. The hunger. The disease.'

It sounded silly even as I said it. What good would crying do? 'I'm sorry,' I said. 'But it all comes out only in your presence.'

'Never mind,' he replied. 'Let it all come out. I still have some tissues left.'

~

In 1962 when Nandini Mehta asked me if I would help at Bal Anand, the school she ran for underprivileged children, I wondered if Krishnaji had had a hand in it. I was delighted to be asked to help but, as I told Nandini, I had no formal training in teaching.

'You like children,' she said. 'That's a very good beginning. The rest you will pick up as you go along.'

'Perhaps I could help them improvise some plays,' I said.

'That's a good place to start,' she replied.

I began with drama but I was soon teaching them painting as

well. I discovered that I did not have any teaching to do. I simply left them alone to produce their masterpieces. I discovered for myself the truth of Pablo Picasso's words, 'Every child is an artist. The problem is how to remain an artist once he grows up.'

Then there were field trips to be taken. We went to Juhu beach together and discovered that when the tide receded, it left behind a huge canvas of undisturbed sand. The children created masterpieces with sticks in their hands as I watched and felt something unwind a little inside me. We went to the circus on another day and then came back to talk about it, to write about it and to draw pictures. Dabboo, one of the little ones who would try and crawl into my lap whenever I sat down, wanted to draw the tigers outside the cages.

When the children wanted to do a play, I told them to go ahead. They would write it, perform it and I would be the audience.

'But what should we write a play about?' one of them asked me.

'Whatever you want,' I replied.

'Shivaji the Great,' said one of the slightly older ones.

'Certainly,' I said.

There followed a great deal of discussion and then a deputation came to me.

'How can we do a play on Shivaji if we haven't even seen a picture of him?' said the leader.

And so the children wrote their own play about the market near the school, putting in the fisherwomen and the noise and the shouting. (Children are always happy if there is a legitimate opportunity to shout.)

I got them magnifying glasses and we went into the garden at Mehta House and studied the flowers and any other biological specimens we could find.

And now three decades later, here I was, in the 'autumn of my life' and here was a girl I had taught.

'I can never forget you,' she said. 'I will always remember how you asked us what we dreamed about.'

I remembered. One little girl almost broke my heart when she said, 'I dream of nimbu paani with ice in it.'

Was it . . .

'I am now a telephone operator here, at St. Elizabeth's,' she said. 'I will try and visit you.'

When she left, I was struck by the coincidences that had brought us together. In a way, we had both left traces in the patterns of each other's lives. Each encounter, I thought, had left something behind in my life. And perhaps I had left something behind too. John Donne's lines came back as I lay in that hospital bed. 'No man is an island,' he had written and then an even more beautiful meditation upon it.

'All mankind is of one author, and is one volume; when one man dies, one chapter is not torn out of the book, but translated into a better language; and every chapter must be so translated . . . As therefore the bell that rings to a sermon, calls not upon the preacher only, but upon the congregation to come: so this bell calls us all . . . No man is an island, entire of itself . . . any man's death diminishes me, because I am involved in mankind; and therefore never send to know for whom the bell tolls; it tolls for thee . . .'

Leela's Epilogue

I can't let this book end without giving my thanks to my dear friends, Adil Jusawalla and his wife Veronik, who prodded and propelled me to writing the book I had in mind. I next got the visit of Adil with a candy-striped fat pencil and matching notebook with an order on page one: 'And now you write.' I stared at the blank page while I sensed that as I proceeded there would be the floes of my personal life's sadness, anxiety, anguish that could so easily crush my book of anecdotes, meant to make the reader of different ages, smile, chuckle and laugh, and sometimes feel the sadness of humanity, past and present.

The night of my blank page, I went to sleep. And then I had a dream (forgive me, a vague echo of Dr Martin Luther King). At nearly five in the morning, I had a waking dream with Jerry Pinto on my lips, loud and clear. I sat on my bed and knew why. I always loved his travelogues, with their sense of humour, his descriptions of landscapes and his sharp pithy descriptions in his film reviews and his own sensitive layers in his poems.

The same morning of my dream I phoned him and said: 'Jerry, could we do a book together?' He was there very soon. I told him that my book would have nothing to do with my life.

Then I said, 'It's only about the funny anecdotes and the sad historic ones I came across.'

Trust Jerry; he returned with his Foreword that I find masterly. And then my first anecdote, chapter one of the book about the six-foot-four Russian. That was a perfect rendition in writing of what I had described orally too; and the other chapters, till Donne's poem to end the book.

My deepest thanks to Jerry Pinto—you are truly my co-author.

~

I end my epilogue with a flurry of wishes for the book; that whoever cares to read it may smile, chuckle and laugh and then understand or feel the sadness, the pain of humanity in certain anecdotes in the historical past and the present.

My wishes go first to my daughter Maya and her son, my grandson, Adam. And then to Erwan, my other grandson—he lost his mother, Priya, my other twin, who had a massive heart attack on 8 February 2008.

Then my wishes go to Catherine, my oldest and dearest friend, her husband Dr Peter Kuhn, their two sons, Mathias and Fabien. Mathias has an older little son—Joshua—and he calls me his Indian dolphin grandmother. He (Mathias) now has a baby son, Benoit, and Fabien has a baby daughter.

How can I forget my dearest friend in India, Pamela Chatterjee and her two daughters who now have children of their own?

Then to those who chose to adopt me as their adopted mother: first Niloufer Karwa, my neighbour above me; then Monica Rosca, a brilliant pianist from Poland and great interpreter of Chopin, who also chose to adopt me as her adopted mother.

To all of you I say, 'adieu'.

Leela Naidu
Mumbai
One grey monsoon morning in July, 2009